RLJ
Publications
Atlanta, GA
USA

The Greater Number

A glimpse of our universe and sort of everything in it

(Or at least a lovely way of looking over it all)

by

Robert Lowe

Featuring

Fabulous Photography
by
George T. Henry

Wonderful Works of Art
by
Crysta Rosella Luke

With Additional fine art by

Patricia Ryan Madson

and

Sophia Sabsowitz

The Greater Number

There is a legend of a great domed temple completely covered
with perfect pearls on the inner surface. The magic was in
the fact that in any single pearl, the entire dome was
visible. Such is the strength of *The Greater Number*
to offer a glimpse of sort of everything in it,
for there is no way to contain even some
of everything; not in all the books, in all
the languages, in all the libraries,
in all the world.

My purpose is to challenge, and titillate
with this gathering of *Word Forms*,
Photography, and Works of Art,
that might encourage flights
of fact, and fancy, and
to support efforts in
learning the deep
wonder of life on
our little planet.

Read through the pages quickly.
Read through the pages slowly.
Read out loud to a loved one;
accepting grammar forms,
punctuating, as carving
tools, for making the
journey pretty.

Requests for permissions addressed to
RLJ Publications
164 4th Street NE, Suite 10
Atlanta, GA USA, 30308
Rlowe46@outlook.com
http://atlantaimprovdocumentary.org

Layout, and Dust Jacket photos by Robert Lowe
Front – Tanah Lot Temple – Bali
Back – Bali Coast

'Word Forms' by Robert Lowe
Photography by George T. Henry
Additional photographs by the author,
by Jonathan Lowe, and by Skydive Atlanta.
Works of Art by
Crysta Rosella Luke
Patricia Ryan Madson, Sophia Sabsowitz, Jonathan Lowe
Elizabeth McCormick Bogue, and AnnLisa Sutton,
Printed in the United States of America.
Available from: Amazon.com, (.CO.UK, .CA, .MX, .DE, .ES, .FR, .AU, .IT, .IN, .JP .IN)
BarnesandNoble.com, abebooks.com, and online world-wide.
(Volume discounts are available from the publisher.)

Dedication

This work is dedicated to my son,
Jonathan Michael Mawle Lowe and to
the next six thousand years.

Contents

Contents (2)

Indebted

To John Steinbeck

In his 1962 Nobel Prize acceptance, he said,

"We have usurped many of the
Powers we once ascribed to God.
Fearful and unprepared,
over the life and death
of the whole world
of all living things.
The danger and
the glory and
the choice
rest finally
in man.
The test of his
perfectibility is at hand."

"Some bad ones there are surely, but by far
the greater number are very good."
The closing line from *A Russian Journal*
by John Steinbeck, 1947

also
Indebted
to the life and work of
Sister Miriam MacGillis

Beginnings

Initially everything
appeared to be inanimate:
mesons, neutrinos, neutron,
proton, electron, electronics,
photon, electromagnetism,
weak, and strong forces,
gravitation,
atom, element,
molecule, colloid, compound,
space, gas of liquid, fire, mineral,
magma, sea waters, atmosphere,
water pure, asteroid, planet, moon,
comet, black hole, star, solar system,
entanglement, pulsar, nebulae, and
probably more than one universe.
Accepting it that our universe has
been 15 billion years in creation,
there had been ten billion years
since that bang so big, that
made up our galactic,
solar system.

Another
two billion years
were expended to come
to the form of Gaia herself.
From molten *magmous* mass,
to conditions, dense and of
sufficient liquid bulk, to
produce an atmosphere
of greenhouse gases:
monoxide carbon,
oxygen, nitrogen,
methane, sulfur,
dioxide carbon.

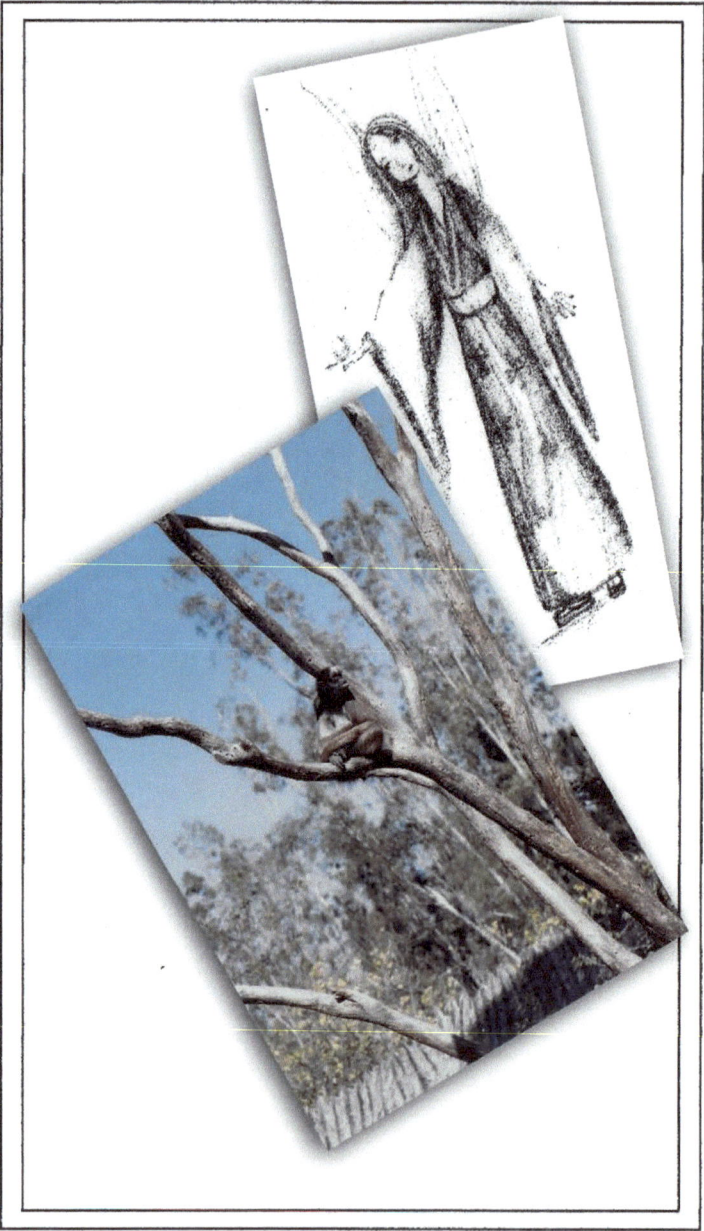

Beginnings (2)

In a Precambrian, saline-mud
there passed another 1.3 billion years
before those gathered greenhouse gasses,
hard and soft metals, alkaloids, and acids,
united by electrons leaping sky to earth,
came to amino acid, nucleic acid,
carbohydrate, and protein,
enzyme and coenzyme.

Tiny bits of bytes were
molded and massaged
by gravity, and tide,
unfathomable time,
extreme pressure,
violent purlieus,
coincidence and,
by many accounts,
mysterious, mystical,
God given processes;
organic, animate
life was born.

Beginnings (3)

This life material
grew in complexity to
matriculate and
mature.
In liquids it played in the
shaping of protein strings,
and viruses, bacterium, and
single celled experiments;
complex chains of volvox.
Chlorophyll arrived and
blue green algae grew
to absorb sunlight,
using it to digest
water and CO2,
freeing more
oxygen.
Arrived also new mediums,
volcanic minerals called
from planetary depths,
pounded by time, and
elements of a spinning
writhing globe.

Ko Kata · Sunset · 3. December 1999

Beginnings (4)

Came the rains
creating glorious
saline substance seas
wherein life exploded into
cells of single prokaryote, monera,
then the oxygen breathing bacteria,
expanding into myriad life assemblies.
Then there were worms,
gelatinoid, cartilaginoid.
Echinoderms followed by
cordata, exo-endo skeletals,
fish, reptiles, and amphibians.
In ancient seas are ichthyosaur,
plesiosaur, and early mammals.

On myriad shores are amphibians.
Developments included massive
extinction; reshaped life paths;
in and upon the living land
bacteria, cast and recast into
more complex organisms.
Ground by living digestion,
there formed fecund topsoil,
and arrival of the wonders:
nematodes, lichen, fungus,
ferns, vines, angiosperms,
plants, trees, biomes,
arachnoids, insects,
reptiles, birds,
marsupials,
mammals,
moles, shrews, rodents, bats,
ruminants, scavengers, and predators.

Beginnings (5)

All this life magic,
Somehow coded, recorded,
Self-regulated. And corrected
evolved, evolved again, reduced,
produced, reproduced, twisted,
sifted, lifted, tossed, and turned
with a double helical dance of
dioxi and ribonucleic acids.
Another 1.6 billion years.
Life progressed toward
complex, to conscious,
to self-consciousness:
whales, anthropoids,
manatees, dolphins,
humans, cats, and such.

Bipedal beings seemed to appear
suddenly, and everywhere on earth,
sometime between four million and
maybe seven million years prior.
Then 4.5 million years,
as our human traces
learned to survive; a
prototype precursor:
Kanapoi hominid.

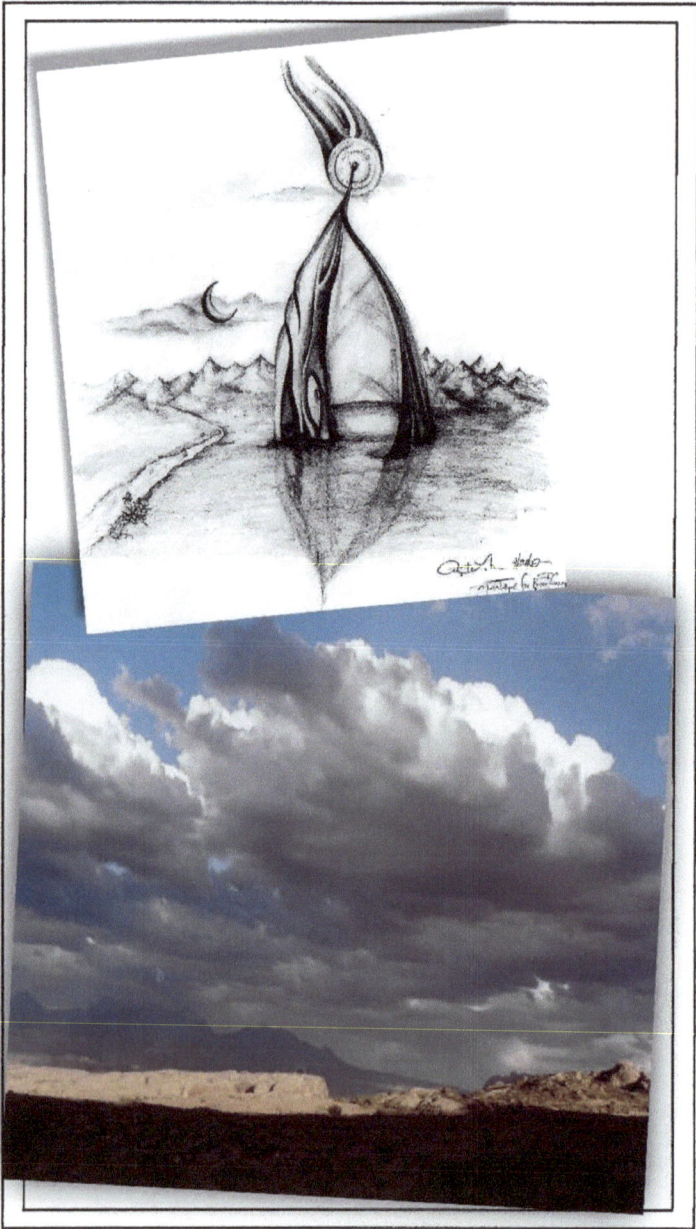

Beginnings (6)

Modern beings
came to be the probable
descendants of the hominids;
climbing trees and walking upright.
Humans, molding, struggled through
Australopithecine;
Lucy, gene mother
of social primates,
three or four million
years before this now.
Then came the scavengers.
Among them, Homo habilis,
sharing semi-permanent camps,
learning the economy of gathering,
2.5 million years before the start of time.
Until eventually in
1,750,00 years,
Homo Erectus
making tools.
Prometheus,
with fire, and
first language.
For another million
and-a-quarter years,
exotic varieties of
hominids walked,
and stalked, then
strode out upon
this tiny globe.

Things we Did and Were

The advent of modern humans may
properly be claimed to have begun as
Neanderthal, and Rhodesian peoples.
These beings seem to
have matured in parallel,
and quite independently
in Africa, Asia, and Europe.
Indications of a revolution
began with the evidence
of ritual burial upon the
fertile crescent & ritual
Iraqi cannibalism at Olduvai,
& Peking Man; the year near 500,000 BCE.
There is a period recorded for us by skeletons,
buildings, wood shelter outlines, from 400,000 BCE,
and flake, and biface tools for chopping from 300,000 BCE.
Neanderthal people are reported around 175,000 years past.
For some time, technology seemed to stand still until Sapiens
migrate out of Africa perhaps 70,000 years in the past, and then
artificial shelters at Orangia in Cape Province by 50,000 BCE.
People certainly crossed Bering Strait before 40,000 BCE,
And beings seeking music made flutes of bear bone.
Homo Sapiens and Cro-Magnon folk
honored medicine people,
and our own sub species,
Homo sapiens sapiens,
made weapons and artifacts:
antler, bone, wood, tusk, stone,
rope, fish hooks, spears hand tools,
as well as baskets, vessels, and icons;
their remnants dated abound 30,000 BCE.
In Lascaux and Trois Freres, humans made
paintings on the walls of caves by 38,800 BCE.
We learned to share our verbal cultural legacies
telling of tales, stories, legends, myths, and rumors.
The first bone needles were used about 15,000 BCE.
Humans appeared on Heiltsuk Island by 12,000 BCE.

Things we Did and Were ₍₂₎

Among these people the first
social and technological
explosion burst forth.
around earth, leading
and resulting in,
accomplishments
extraordinaire.
This Neolithic Revolution,
birthed some 12,000 years past,
carried on for six thousand years or so,
resulted in the domestication of animals:
dogs by 12,000 BCE, sheep by 9,000 BCE;
and cattle made tame, earth made sense.
Also came creation of pottery from muds
by Jomon, Japanese, around 10,500 BCE.
Tombstones and massive earthworks
were our first architectural footprints.
evidence of Egyptian buildings by 9000 BCE,
& bundled reed fences, as well, by 7500 BCE.
Natufians made bird bone flutes near 7000 BCE.
They had eight holes, tuned to a minor third
interval, and are able to be played today.
The period then introduced cultivation,
and tending of previously wild crops,
the spinning and weaving of cloth,
the development of metallurgy;
copper beads and trinkets
in Turkey near 6,500 BCE.
With no durable records,
for another 6,000 years
civilization disperses
from early beginnings
of the Neolithic revolution,
until the invention of record keeping.
We have been writing for only half as long
as we have been living as more than animals.

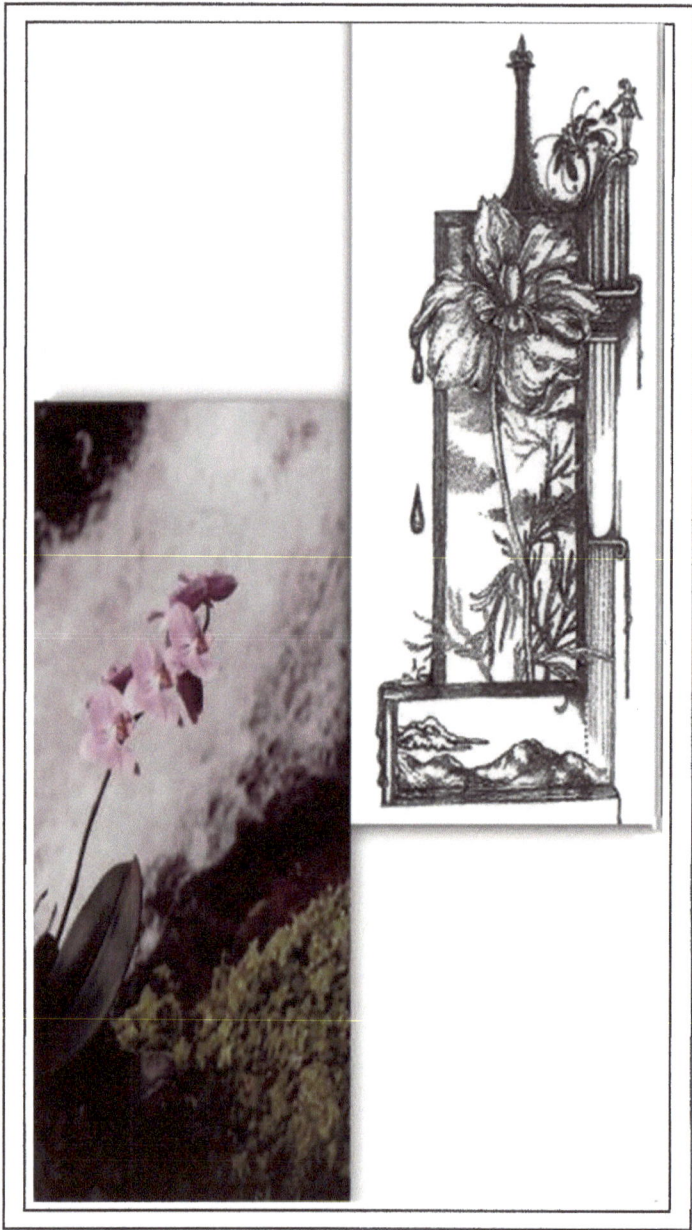

Things We Did and Were (3)

During our unrecorded years
we walked across the earth,
floated upon the water, &
probably took to the sky
in balloons of hot air.
As we domesticated
many grains, and animals,
we domesticated each other as well.
We apparently created and discovered
such wonders as complex languages, tools,
fishing, boat building, agriculture, fired clay,
landscaping, sculpture, poetry, music, dance,
animal husbandry, building technology,
art, intricate pottery, architecture,
religion, industrial design,
and philosophy.

We found wisdom in
many rituals, ceremonies,
festivals, oracles, fertility cults,
Fu Hsi, Quan Yin, Budo, Wicca, and
Chou I - I Ching – the Book of Changes.
Humans created stone megaliths,
priesthoods, administrations,
bureaucracies, politics,
myths, and ziggurat.
We engaged in vast
irrigation and mining efforts,
creating and using, numbers,
arithmetic, algebras, and geometries,
spinning, weaving, linen making, and
the use of bows and arrows,
leading to drystone huts
at Ain Mallaha, Israel.

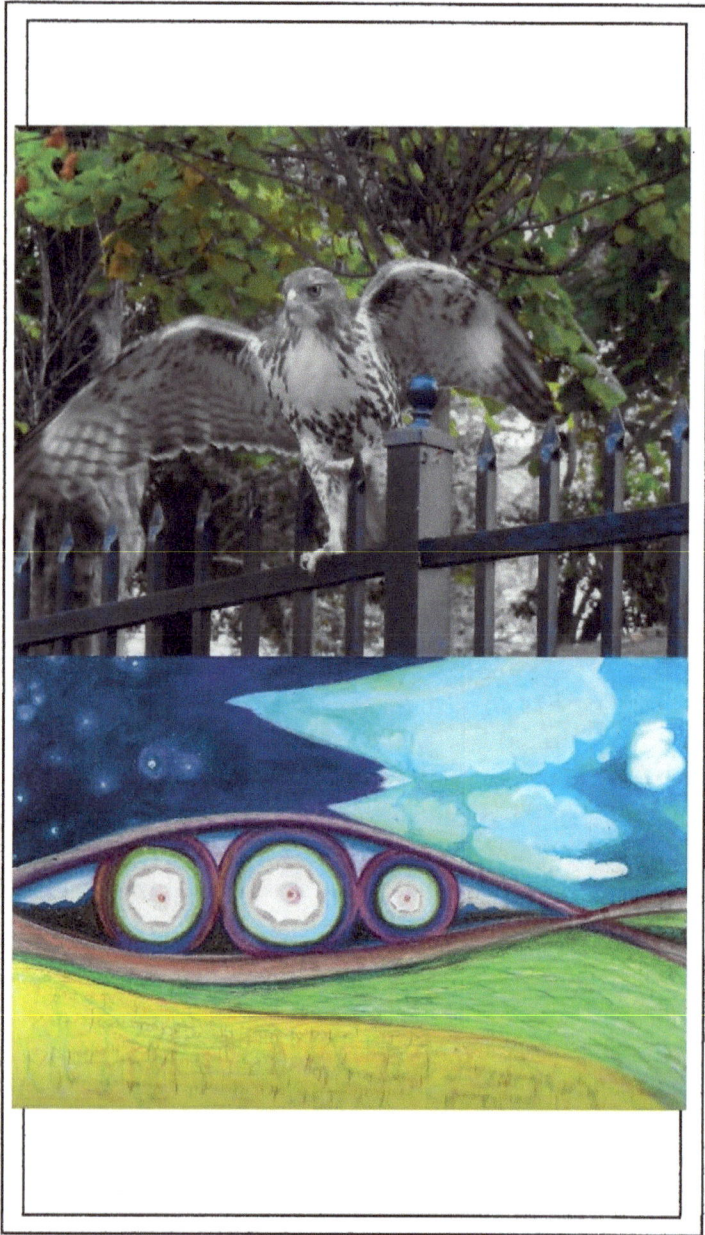

Things We Did and Were

Humans engaged in commerce
evolving manifold trade routes.
Residential buildings appeared.
Jericho was founded by 10,000 BCE;
beehive forms, and stone paved floors.
By 8,000 BCE we find the city was graced
by a population of 2,000. It also had finished
lime plaster, and red ochre paint. Housing and
village formats, left for us footprints on the earth:
huts, lean-tos, pit-houses, timber framed houses,
Longhouses, Drystone houses, collective tombs.
There is a 166 -foot tumulus
barrow downs at Gordon;
megalith passage-graves,
and grave galleries and
earthen longbarrows.
By 6,000 BCE the town of Catal Hüyük,
in Turkey, supported a population of 6,000.
Matter is known as earth, air, fire, and water.
Shrines were found at Djeitun and Pessejik,
then temples at Tell-es-Sawwanand, Iraq.
Following came funerary architecture.
A thousand-year age of copper began.
The wheel appeared by 4,000 BCE,
and in Egypt we conceived of
the 'Divinity of Kings'.
Before recorded history began
myriad cultures were unfolding.
We are blessed to know of families:
the Sumerians, Danubian Europeans,
Yang Sha, Lung Shan, and Jarbu Chinese;
Bitterroot Americans, Maghreb Africans,
those called Banthu, Kalahari, Hodza, Ituri;
Thai, Egyptians, the Anasazi, Cochise,
then the Ova Tjimba stone makers
living in North West Africa,
and Afro-Mediterraneans,
and the Mechta el Arbi;
all before 'history'.

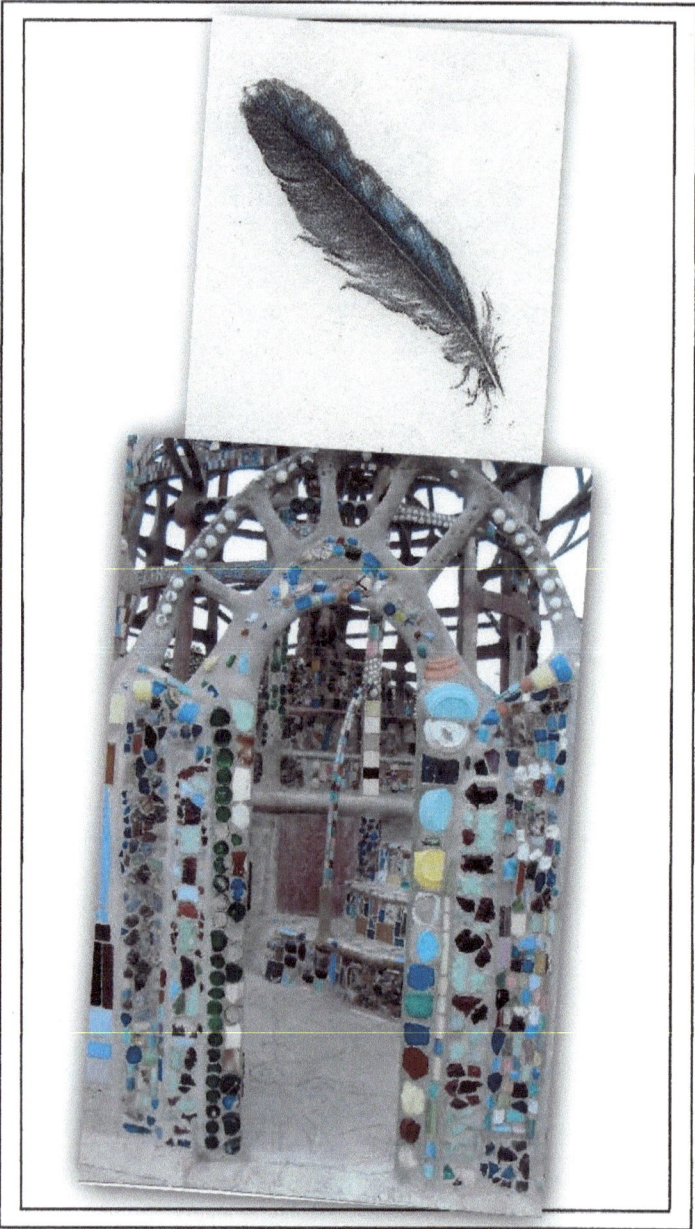

Participants Known to Me

My grandparents were
each born before 1900.
A grandfather came to
America from England,
while another sailed on
the Charles W. Morgan,
America's only surviving
whole wooden whaler.
Grandmothers both
traveled Conestoga
to America's west.

None of their children were
educated beyond the 10th
grade, yet they lived most of
their lives among the earth's
first generation of non-royal
humans fairly secure in
believing that daily needs
could & might be met.

Prior to my grandparent's generation
almost every being of humanity lived
essentially in search of sufficient
food, shelter,
and succor
to survive
by the day,
or perhaps,
the season.

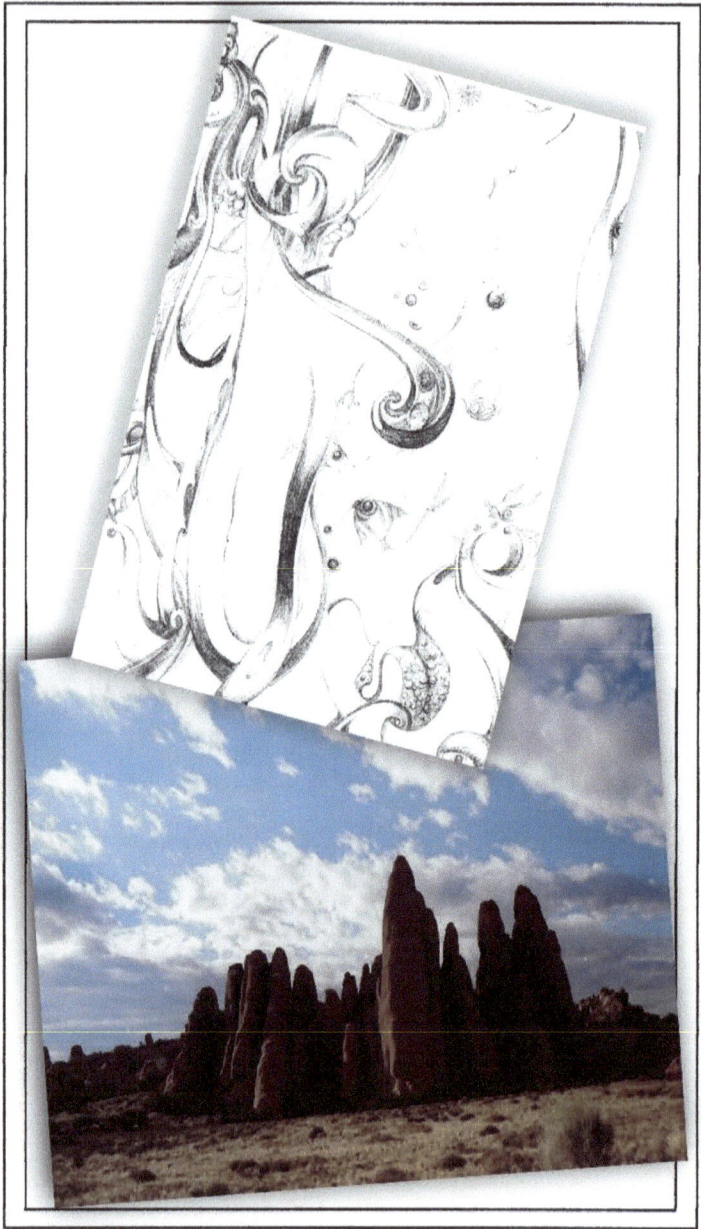

War. Depression. War.

My parent's generation,
were to become known as
the first human generation
somewhat able, to produce
and secure future needs for
large numbers of people.

This was more or
less true world-wide,
beside severely declining
levels of prosperity among
economically suppressed and
undeveloped populations.

Through a second World War,
and into the 1960's, building
and retooling occurred,
at unprecedented pace;
massive development.
Effort for the future
and human security
became a hallmark
of the generation.

We Came Next

My generation,
characterized by some
as the baby boomers,
born during an
18-year period
beginning truly
about May of 1946,
roughly nine months
after the Japanese surrender
that ended World War II.

We, arrivals of a baby boom,
are among the first generation
of conscious beings raised with
the primal assumption
that the needs of today,
and tomorrow
shall be met.

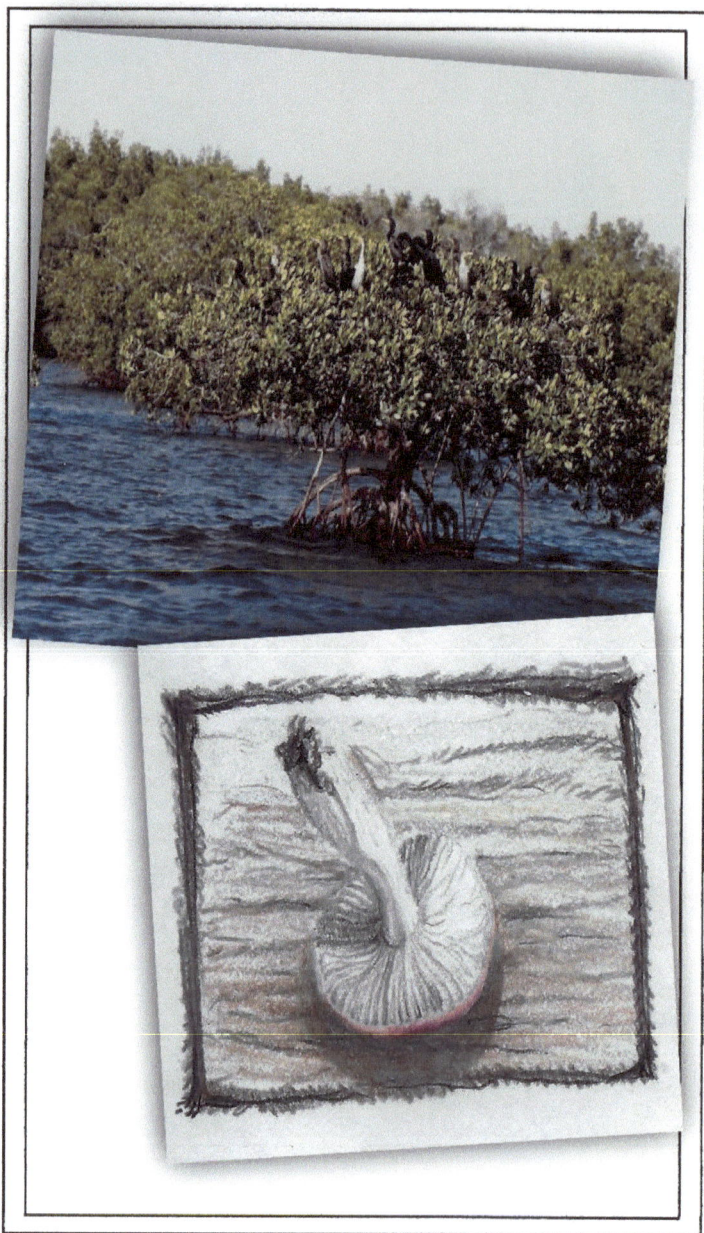

We Came Next (2)

Those having been born
between 1964, and today,
variously called such as
generations x, y, www;
unknown, too soon to tell.
These folks have been born
into an explosive chaos of
creation and exploration,
information, perspective,
development, invention,
unheard of options,
hope, fear, surplus,
waste, & miracles.
Yet we have also
grown with the fear
of nuclear destruction,
cancers, random terrorism,
ecological & biological disaster,
among the bitter reminders
of the transience of life.
Focus on the present
becomes the hallmark
of these generations.

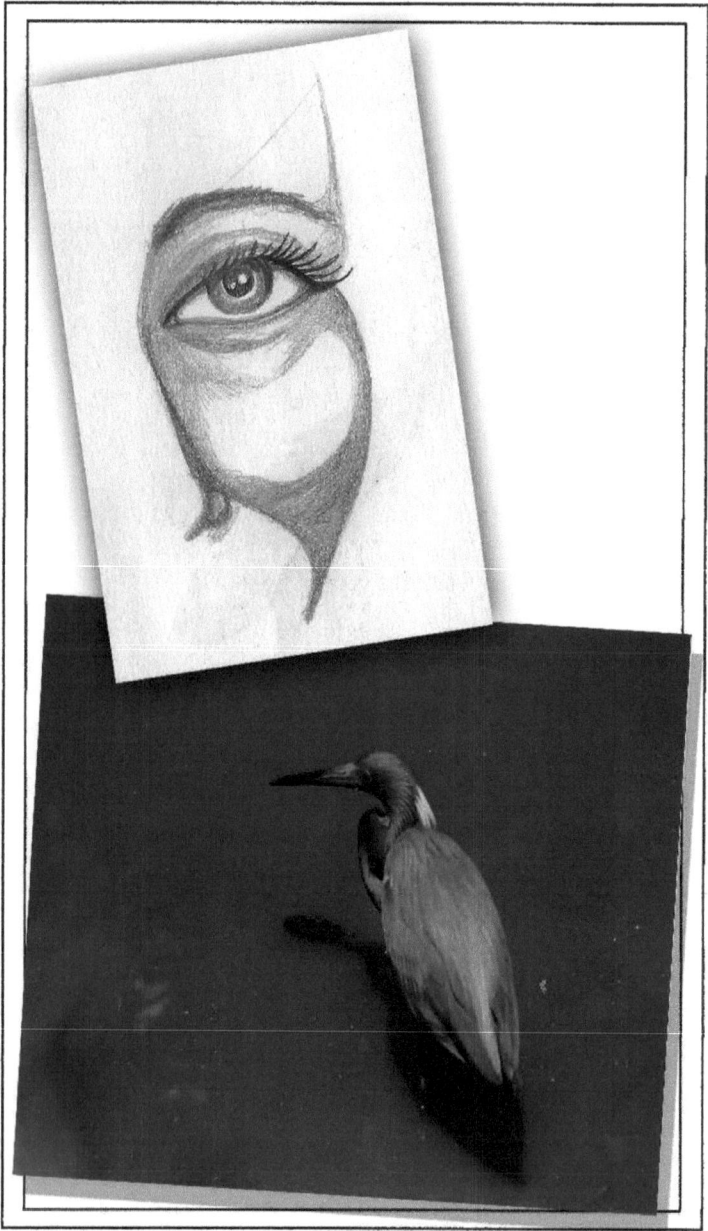

We Came Next (3)

Beneath the wealth
there continue to be deep
survival and comfort disparities
between the industrial world
and undeveloped regions,
countries, and enclaves.
The greater majority of
the world population
continues to exist
in a poverty,
living from
day to day,
perhaps season to season,
storm to storm, flood to flood,
earth quake to volcano eruption,
new famine, to plague, to war;
this neither more nor less
than the normal state
of human life as it
was before my
grandparent's
generation.

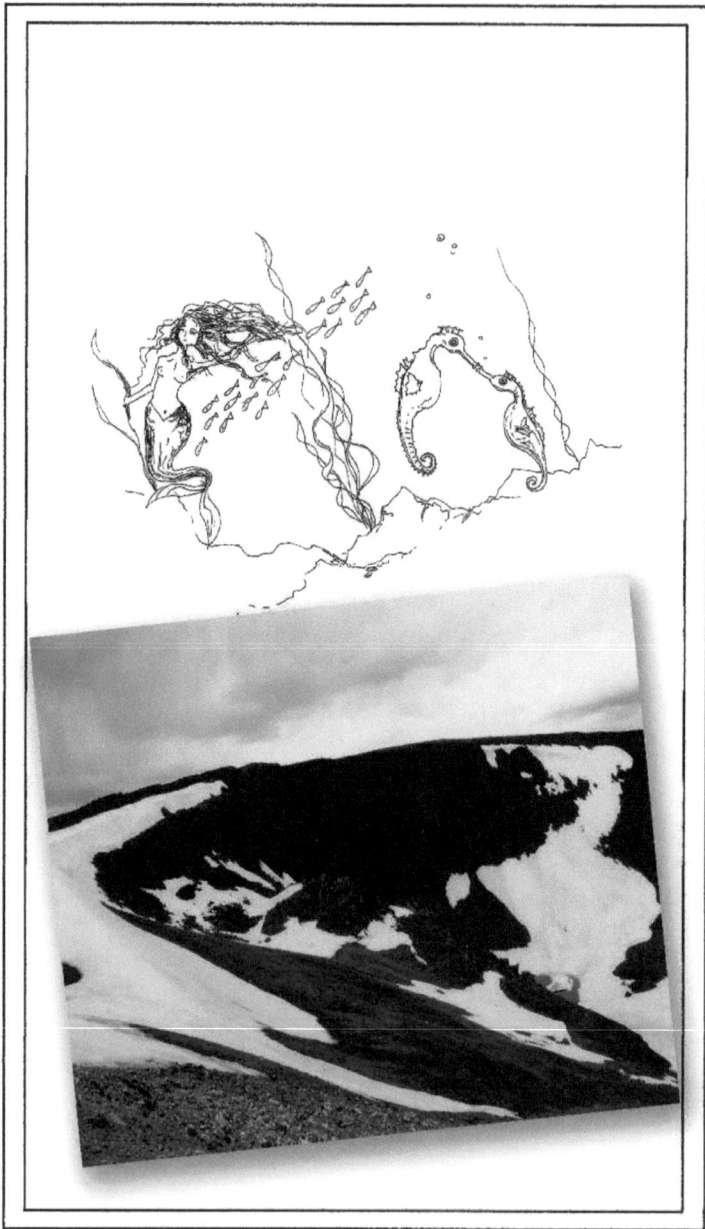

This Time Now

We live in an era
of quantum change.
This new change is as
massive a modulation as
took place when life first
presented upon the earth;
as massive a modification
occurred at the advent of
consciousness, and again
upon the beginnings of
civilized cooperation.

There is a change
more intense than
experienced in
Neolithic
revolution,
ages of gold,
and of copper;
of Africa, Asia,
Rome, or China,
Renaissance, and
industrial revolution.
The revolution of our time
eclipses the electronic, the atomic,
the sub-atomic, the cosmic, new age,
and information revolutions.

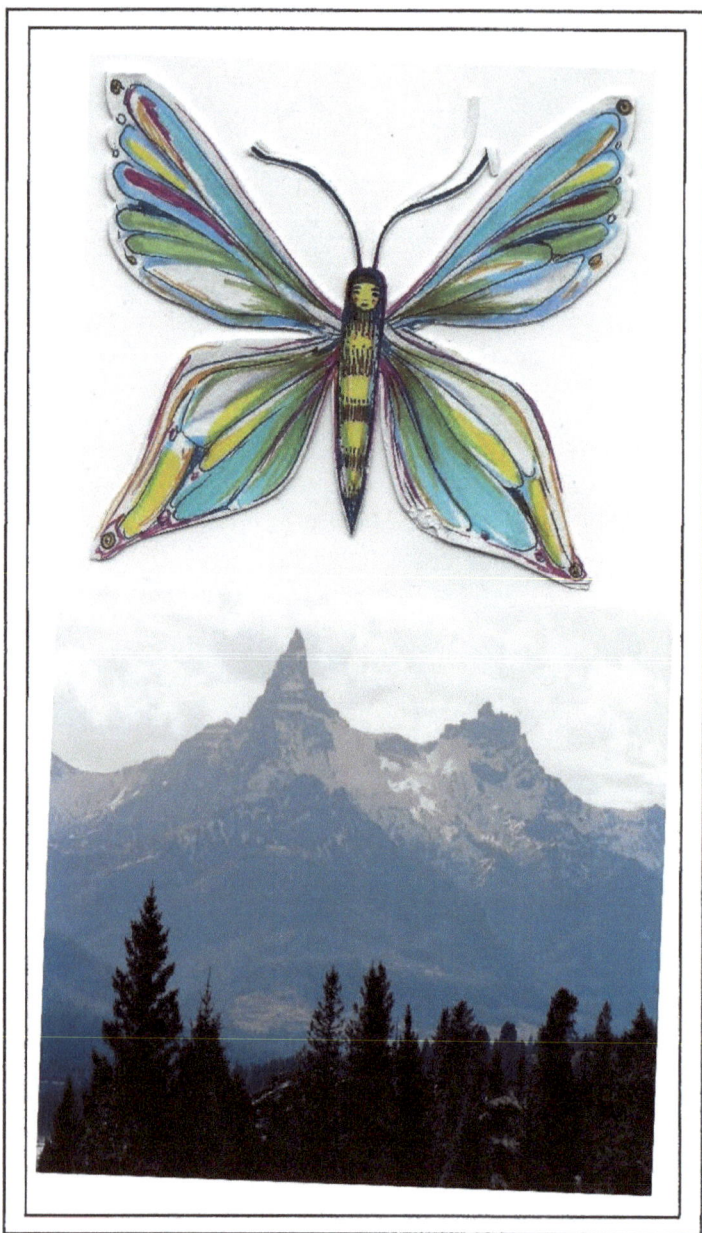

This Time Now (2)

For all of time
it was only Gaia
made new things.
During most of the years
of humanoid existence
fire was an exclusive
province of nature.
Fully in her hands,
were management of land,
and water, and the length and depth,
and beginnings, and endings of life.

In recent time
many of the essential
activities of the world
have been removed
from earth guided,
automatic pilot;
are being taken
into the hands
of populations
and of humans.

Responsibility
for fundamental
life events are being
now guided by, oh so
frail human beings,
and by our, all too
human, minds.

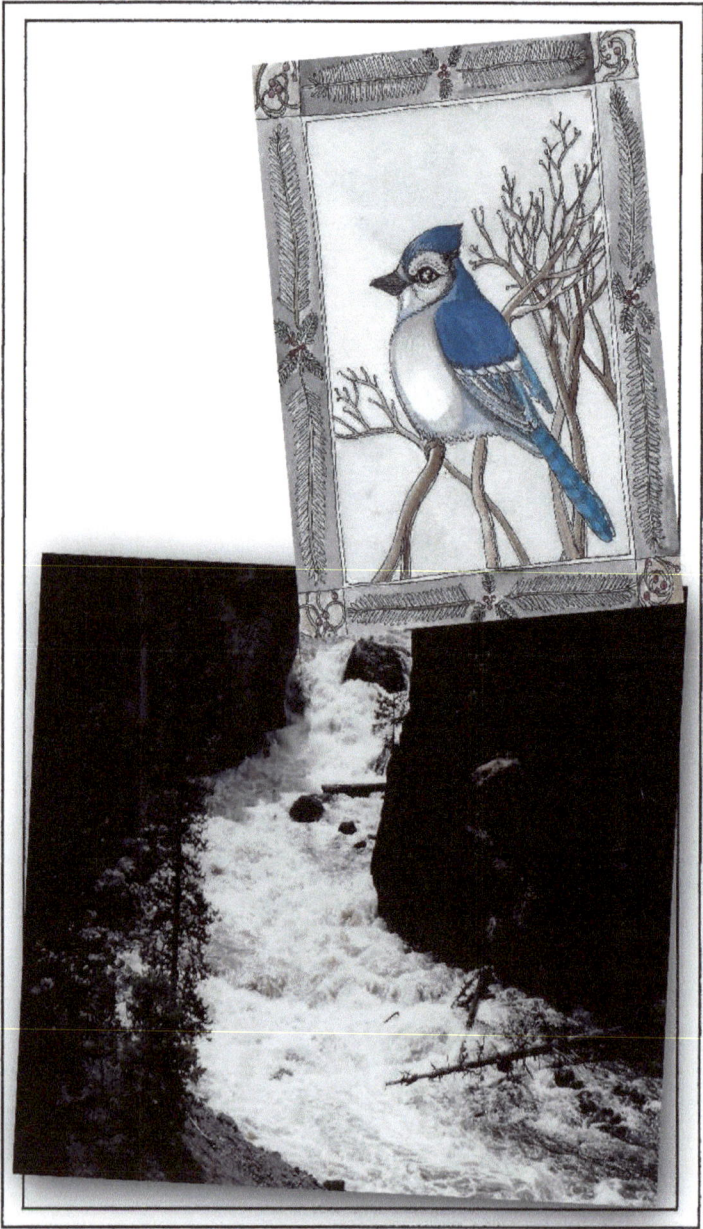

This Time Now (3)

From Copernicus
to Galileo, Kepler,
Newton, and then
on to the most recent
26 human generations,
500 years on average,
human intervention
and manipulation
has culminated in
the storming of
provinces
of nature.
Areas into
which we have
made interventions
show: mechanics as heat,
and heated steam management,
use of plastics, light technologies,
mechanical and structural engineering,
metal tooling, and micro measurements,
quantum optics, photo chemicals, lazars,
manipulated electromagnetic frequencies;
short wave, radio, TV, microwave miracles;
sound recording, reproduction, ultrasound,
SCUBA, deep water submergence,
petrochemical technology,
sonic surgery and therapy,
genetic engineering,
nuclear technology,
and subatomic
creations.

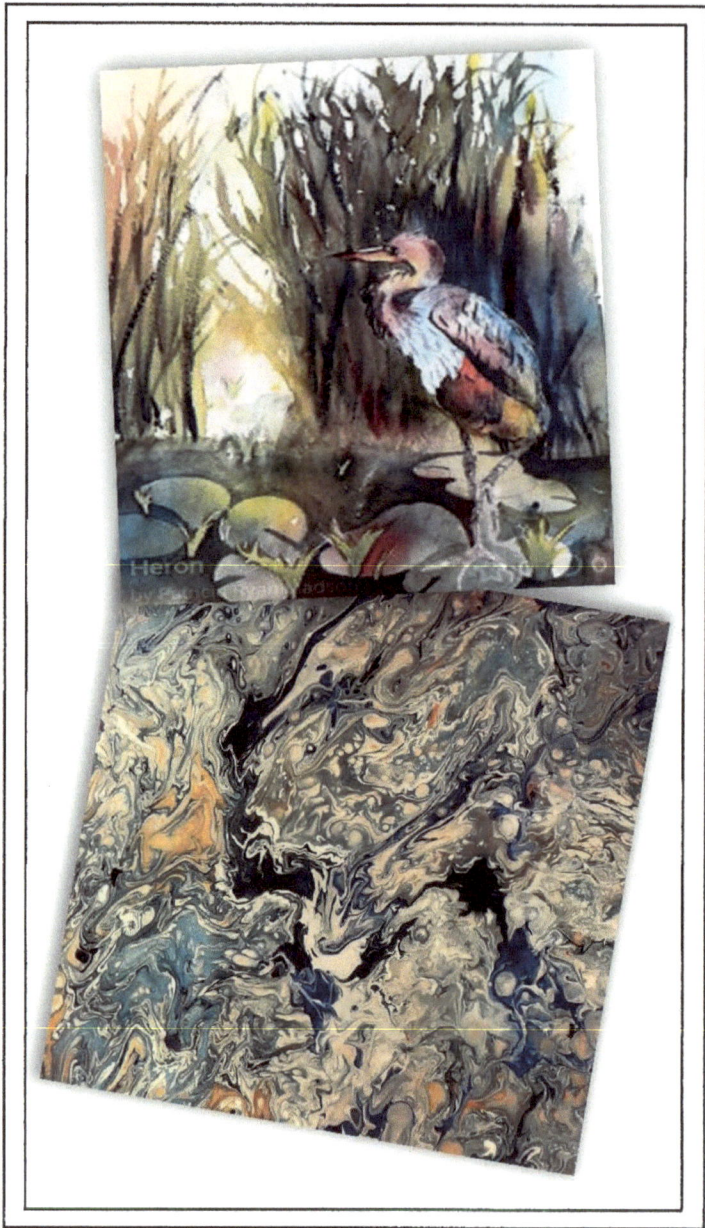

This Time Now (4)

We have engaged in
the creation of elements:
Neptunium, numbered 93,
to Meitnerium, recorded 109,
and then on to the number of 118.
There are miraculous bio-wonders:
lifelike prosthetics, biochemistry,
surgeries, and organ transplants.
We have explosives, fuels, and
fertilizers, and near mystical
compound technologies:
alloys, pharmaceuticals,
glass building construction,
computer memory, fiber optics,
incendiaries, silicon technology.
Humans have developed optics:
telescopy, electron microscopy,
magic video, copying, and email.
We have ceramic technologies with
temperature controls, and magnetics.
Environmental comprehensions include
weather, and global climate awareness,
and planetary ecology manipulation.
We have probed the sky, the oceans,
the lands and mountains as well as
space, anti-space, anti-time,
crystal technologies,
virtual reality, and
anti-matter.

In these, and more,
humans march forward
taking over management of
ancient and natural events.
It is in this field of play
in which we transit
a 21st Century.

This Time Now (5)

As the
fundamental
aspects of life come
under our controls,
we are presented
with a question
as to whether
we can learn
to act
as responsible participants
in an ancient progression
of life, and the expansion
of conscious existence,
and can take our place
to carry life forward;
or whether we will
bring to an end
our days of
being.

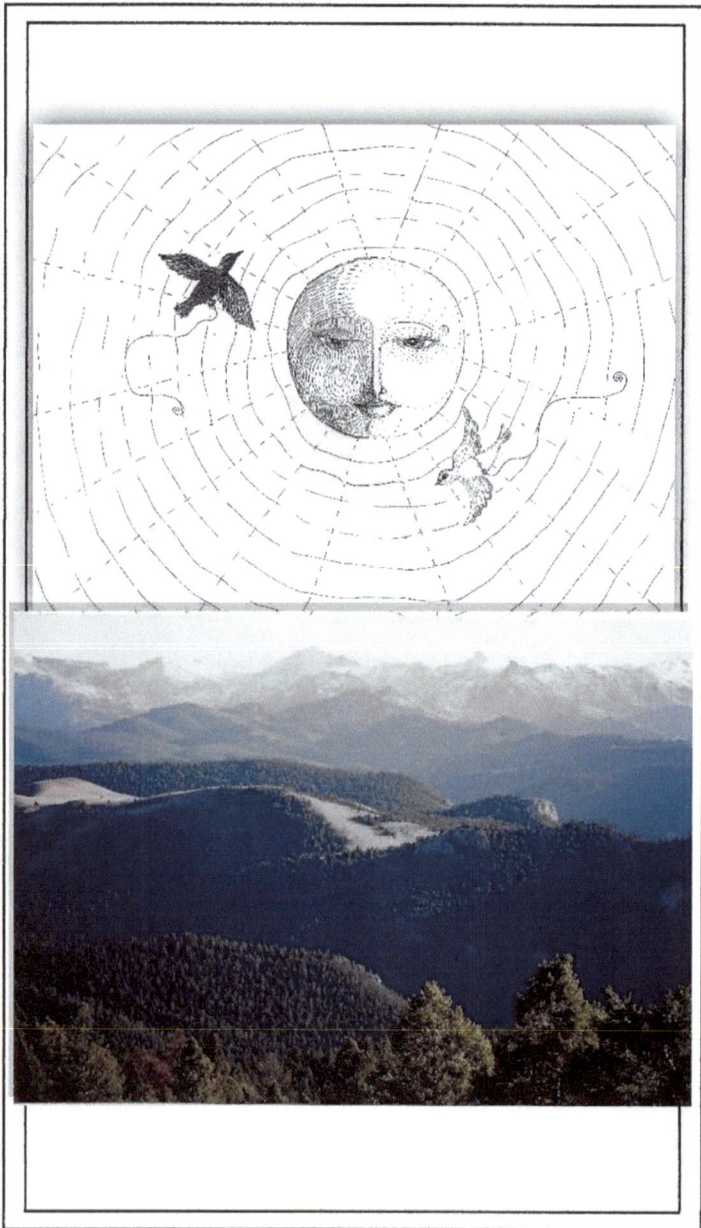

A Time Perspective

To form a
working grasp
of the panoply in
the miracle of time
it is perhaps helpful
to reduce the days to
relative measurements.
Carl Sagan once proposed
this metric of compression.

If 'humans' appeared these 500-millennium past,
and we use our very young minds to compress
these half million years into one single day,
the first twenty-three and one-half hours
can be viewed as a great tribal period
about which we know very little.

Our megaculture's time upon the stage
began with that Neolithic revolution,
of a dozen thousand years ago, and
the few recordings of our history
scribbled some 6000 years past.

We can compress all recorded
messages of our experience
into a thirty-minute frame.
With this perspective we
can know one thousand
years as though being
under three minutes.
Two hundred years
can become half a
minute, and one
year passes by
in just a fifth
of a second.

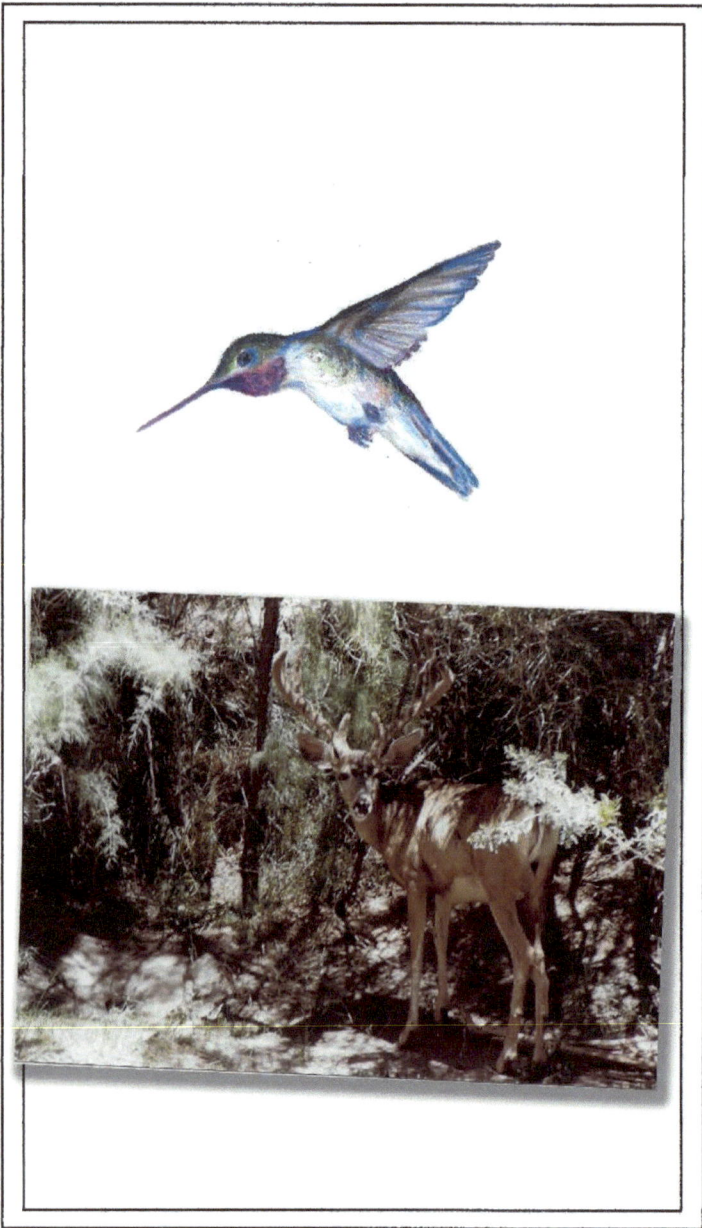

This Record

The items in these *Word Forms*
are intended to scramble a strict chronology.
Event, impact and development are, however,
all gathered within the given time brackets.
Within the ranges, the people and things,
inventions, thoughts, philosophies, and
entries are quite loosely associated;
by whimsy set beside one another,
sometimes only to allow a shape.
Reflective meditation guides
came to my heart and mind,
often with great random
happenstance: cultures,
discoveries, events,
ironies, realities,
and peoples;
more magically linked
than calendars allow.

Hope is that this book
may be used as a working
guide, reference, and checklist.
Should you find anything of which
you would wish for more knowledge,
seek it out. Find meaning for yourself.
For now, relax and read on.
Forgive me for omissions.
May this poem of time
roll past your mind
as time rolls
past us all.

Take note that in our time
life had been upon earth for
1.5 billion years,
or more.

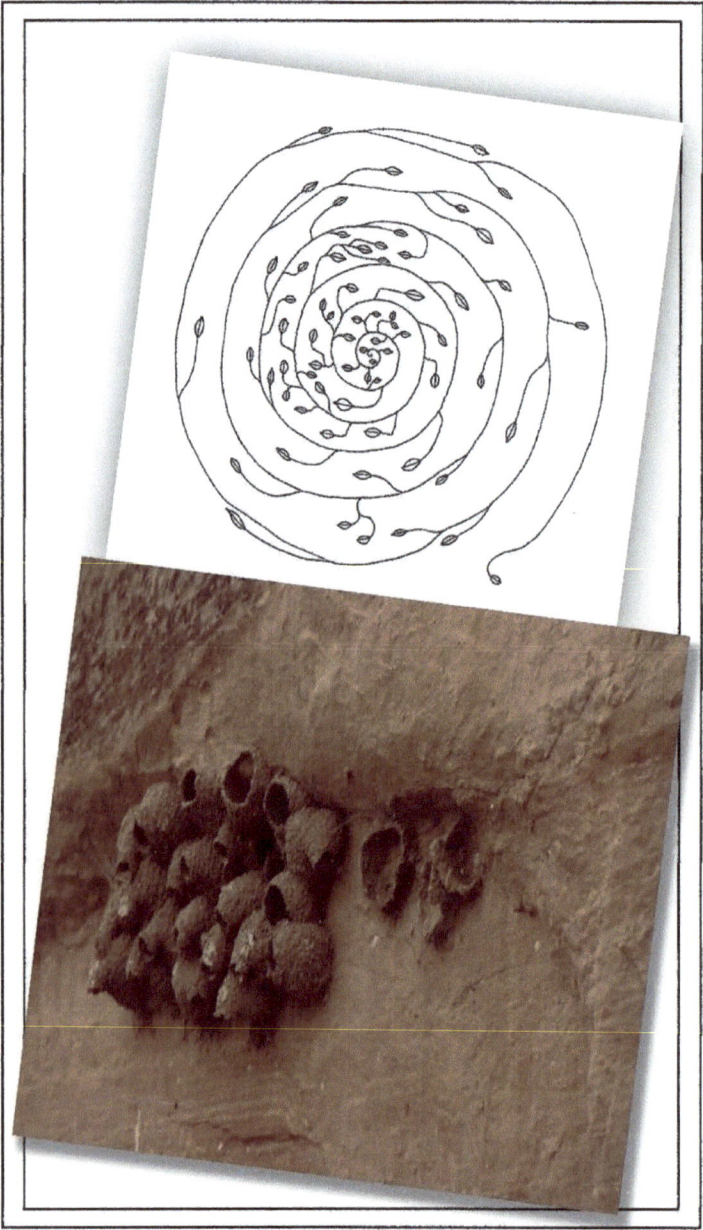

4000 to 3000
Before the Common Era

Merely 17 Minutes ago,
within this millennium,
a Judaic calendar tells us that
recording of time began in 3760 BCE.
First writing is in the Sumerian city of Uruk;
'syllabary' words of ownership on clay seals,
with pictographs on copper artifacts, and
notation on Tigris, and Euphrates clays.
Viewing these human records, we see
sail boats, galleys, wheeled vehicles,
potter's wheels, kilns, flint mining,
irrigation systems, traction plows,
bread making, beeswax candles,
copper smelting, bronze tools,
plus, weaving with looms.
There are straw skirts,
and leather shoes.
Our Ziggurats include:
Tchoga-Zanbil, in Elan,
the White Temple at Ur.
Egyptian civilization expands
including columns and capitals,
gracing an Upper, and Lower Nile.
temples of Henthotep, Ggantija.
Ammon Amun appears at Luxor
where Amenosphis III built, and
a lost Punt culture is trading.
British megaliths are created,
and columns are built from
images suggested by
stalks of vegetables.
We have the lever.

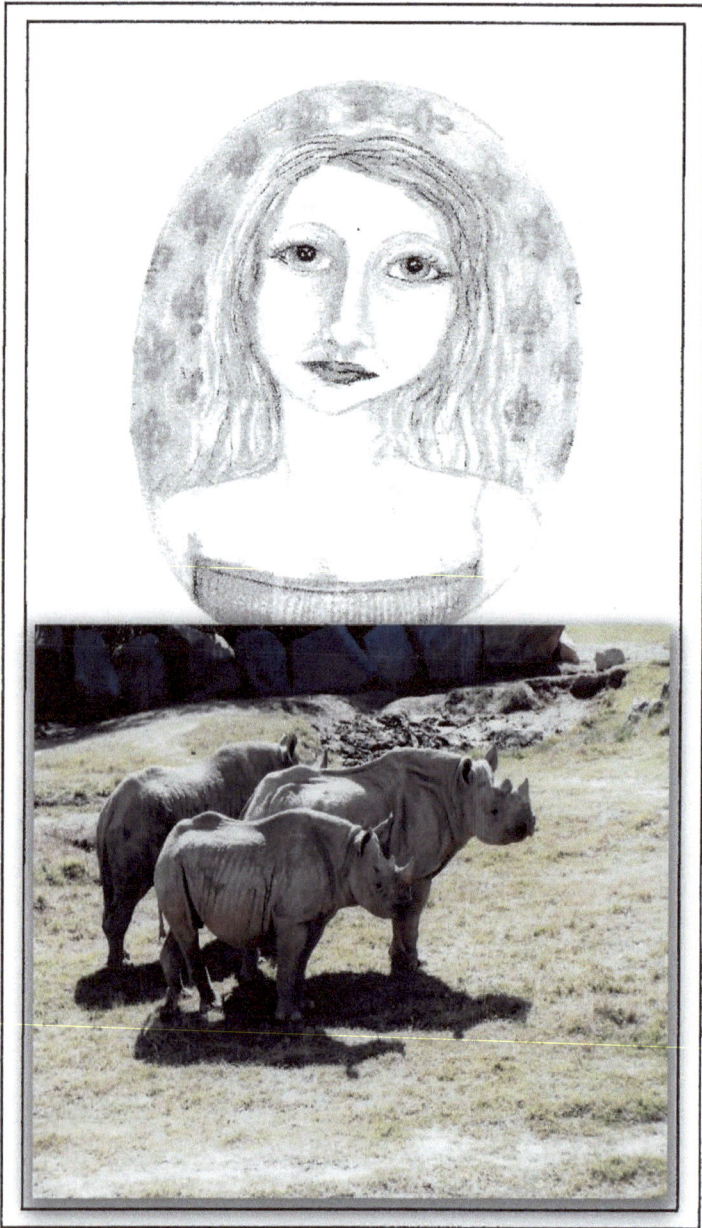

4000 to 3000 BCE (2)

The Earth Goddess, Ninna appears,
and Mesopotamia has a council of gods.
Salicylate pain relieving plants are used.
Divination is being accomplished using
dreams and interpretation of entrails.
There are terra cotta clays,
earliest wine making works;
along with Isis, Osiris, and Ra.
The Breaker culture germinates
in central Europe, while city states
emerge, grow, and develop to the south.
Cretan Minoans, and Phoenicians appear.
People build the foundation of Troy.
Armenian Kura-Araxes arise.
We record the beginning of
farming in the Indus valley.
Mandingo culture in Sierra Leone,
and a Mayan Calendar gives dates to
Chilica Peruvians, and Ecuadorian pottery.
There are Cuneiform script, Hieroglyphics,
and metal-molding chariots,
as well as a harp, and lyre.
The world Population is
guessed to have been
ten million.

3000 to 2000 BCE

In California mountains
Bristle cone pines are born.
Peoples discover and form
the bases of antiphonal music,
cosmetic implements, and hereditary kings.
While Sumerians create The Gilgamesh Epic,
Elbans and Indus Valley civilizations emerge.
There is a granary and bath at Mohenjo-Daro.
Imhotep, as the first architect to be recorded,
designs the Stepped Pyramid of King Zoser.
We expand our written communication to
proto-Indian script, and Akkadian script.
As the Aryan Persian culture appears,
Montana cave drawings are created,
Assyrians and Babylonians emerge,
and there is the first pottery
in North America.
In China is the
Beginning of an
Age of Five Emperors
Plano-convex brick is invented.
Sakkara Step Pyramids are built.
An Age of Bronze and metallurgy
begins; humans develop central
governments, pyramids, and
the Sphinx in Egypt, though
some may dispute her age.
We extend our temples
with henges and
burial mounds,
enclosures, &
causeways.

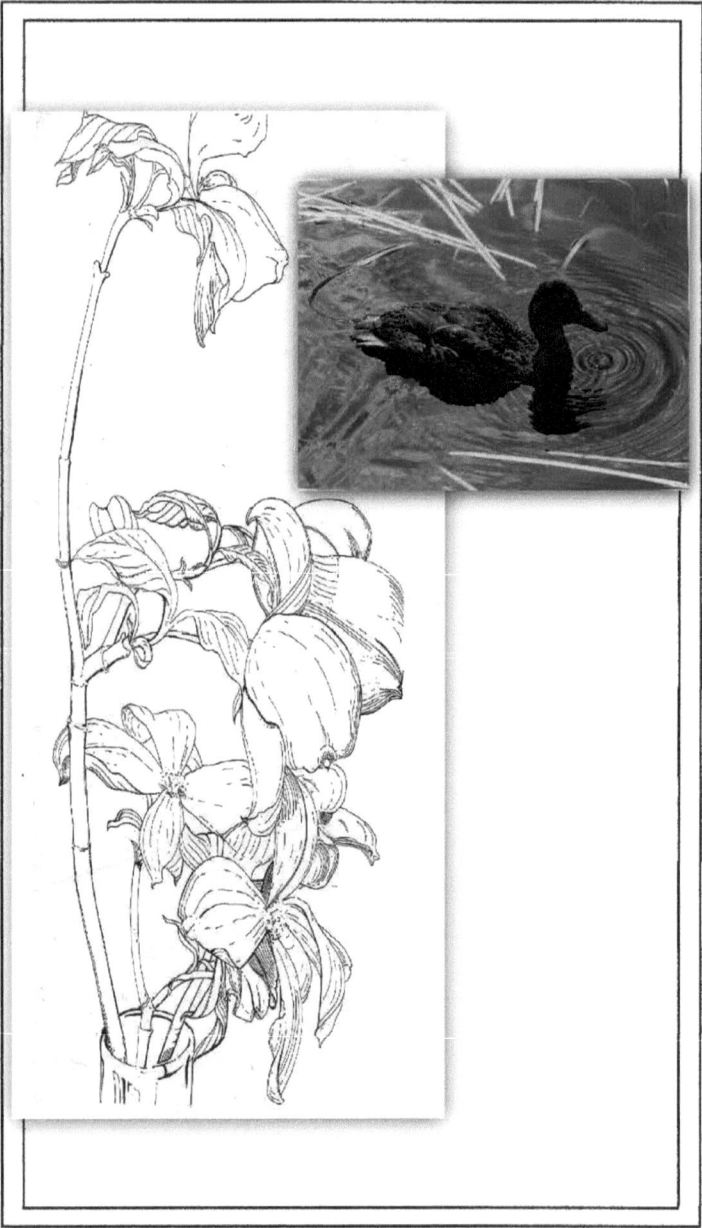

3000 to 2000 BCE (2)

We build fortifications and stone towers,
A-frame buildings, and corbeled arches,
use weight standards, and plumb lines.
The divine king of record is Naramsin.
The first code of law appears in Ur.
Tan Gun establishes Korea.
Yangshao China emerges
with 'concept' script.
See the Thai bronzes.
Acupuncture is in use,
and papyrus documents.
Decorated ceramic ware is used,
as are horse drawn wheeled vehicles.
Sewerage and drainage systems are in cities.
Medical diagnosis and treatments are established,
and Nevada duck decoys, and a 365-day calendar;
meanwhile we also experience end blown flutes,
double reed flutes, and soldering technique.
In Egypt there are first clowns, jesters, and
Coronation Festival plays; ritual dramas.
The Great Pyramid complex gives us
Cheops, Chephren, Mykerinus;
the beginnings of Stonehenge,
the first library in Babylon.
Recording of war begins
in Mesopotamia.

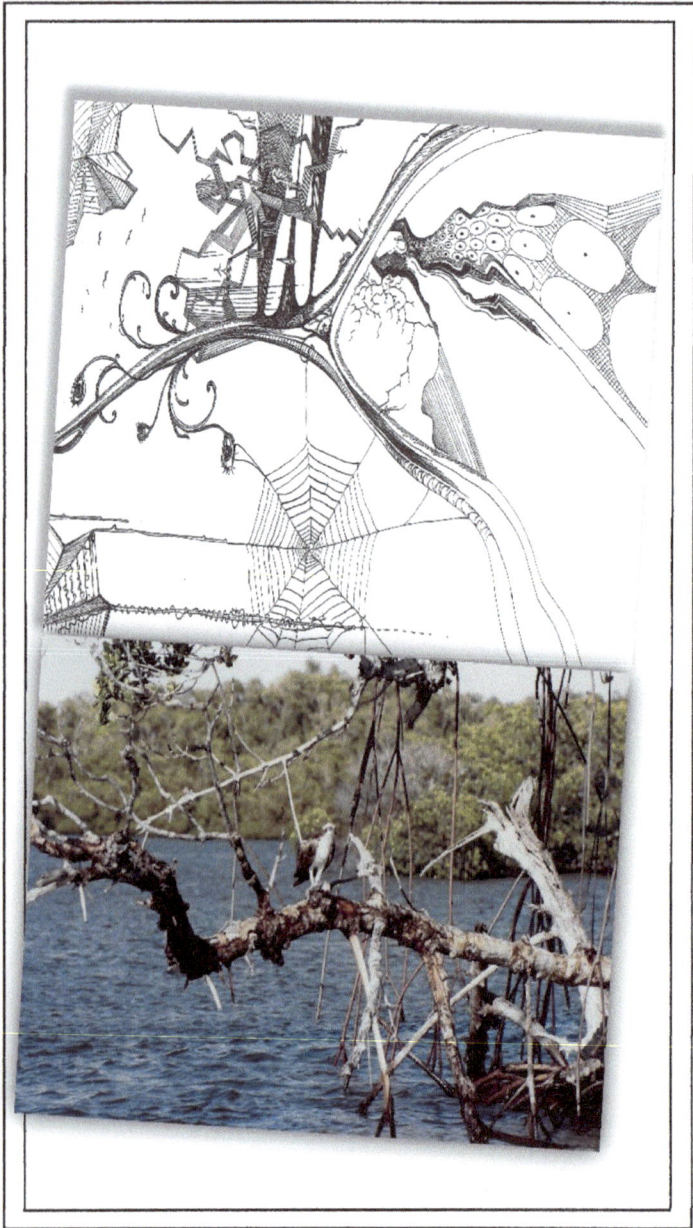

2000 to 1000 BCE

Begins the Age of Iron,
timber, drystone, hill
forts, & fortified buildings.
Pottery is up on wheels, and
humans engage in carpentry.
Here comes the beginning of
3,900 years of slave societies.
There are 'Linear A' syllabic scripts,
general manufacturing, and walled cities;
Babylonia, Hammurabi, and young Troy.
King Wen begins a great consolidation
of China. There appear first recordings of
Tai Chi, and Karate begin to develop, as do
calligraphy, Origami, and tea ceremony.
There are Xia, and Shang Chinas,
Zhou to last for eight hundred years.
In Central America are ceremonial
temples revealing architecture.
Chin philosophy develops.
The first consonant scripts:
alphabetic writing in Syria,
the Phonetic alphabet, and
a Greek alphabet are begat.
Great circles and megalithic
stone forms, grace the earth.
A Phoenician state flourishes.
The giant redwoods are seeded.
Jewish civilization expands, and
Moses stands with God at Mt. Sinai.
See sun dials, glass, and fresco painting.
The scientific study of astronomy grows
with Babylonians. Lydia precedes Turkey.

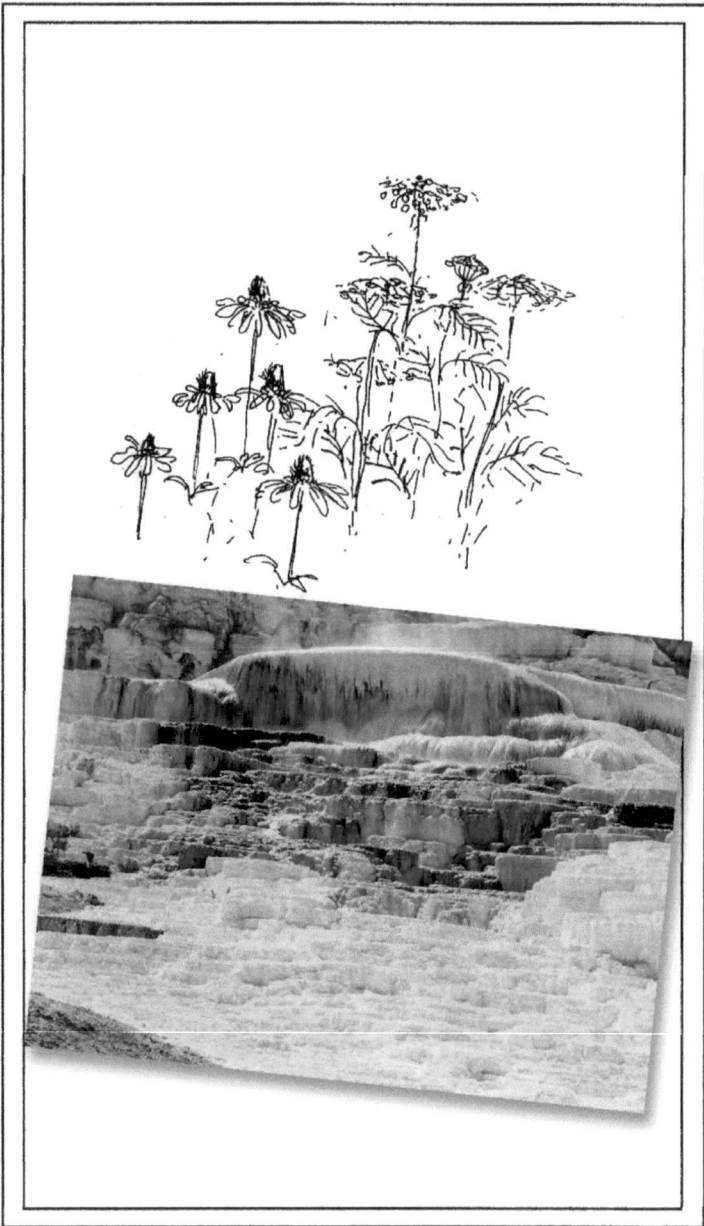

2000 to 1000 BCE (2)

In Peru we construct temples.
Uses of bronze metalwork expands.
Etruscans develop exceptional beauty in
artistry with gold, statuary, burial sites, and
Improvisational theatre, through *The Atellana*.
In Wucheng Sichuan, China, the first Dinosaur
fossils are discovered and called 'dragon bones'.
Wessex England, and Celtic Europe expand.
Tang turns into Jin China, to last 900 years.
We witness the water clock, purple cloth,
glass bottles, international commerce,
Canaanites, Aramaens, Philistines.
Egyptian toss juggling, love songs;
and we know of Passion Plays.
Theatre is born, and matures
in the New Kingdom,
and there is the
Book of the Dead.
Marionettes appear.
Senmut designs a temple
for his Queen Hatshepsut,
the solitary female pharaoh.
The Greeks build Lion Gate.
There is a Treasury of Atreus,
largest ever free interior space.
King Mino's palace is at Knossos.
Kassite peoples conquer Babylon.
Numbering systems are complex
tables have squares, square roots,
whole numbers and fractions; and
tablet records, and 'Linear B' script,
cubic equations, exponential functions,
Hurrian Hymn #6 is our first written music.

2000 to 1000 BCE (3)

Hindu theology emerges; also
a Rig Veda, hymns, and chants.
Trojan wars record battles at sea.
Humanity produces Tutankhamun,
a foundation of civilization by laws,
and large-scale military organizations.
Assyrians dig tunnels with metal chisels.
Disease is approached by examination,
diagnosis, prognosis, and treatment.
We are Olmec Mexicans, Mayans,
Hittites, Mycenaeans, and
Glacial Kame Americans.
Feudal political structures develop,
as we introduce the first coinage,
fretted finger boards on the lute,
iron smelting, sharpened iron,
North American canoes, and
the first saddles and reins;
preserved fish for food,
cementation steel, and
there are trumpets of
copper and of silver;
a pentatonic scale.
An oracle speaks
at Delphi.

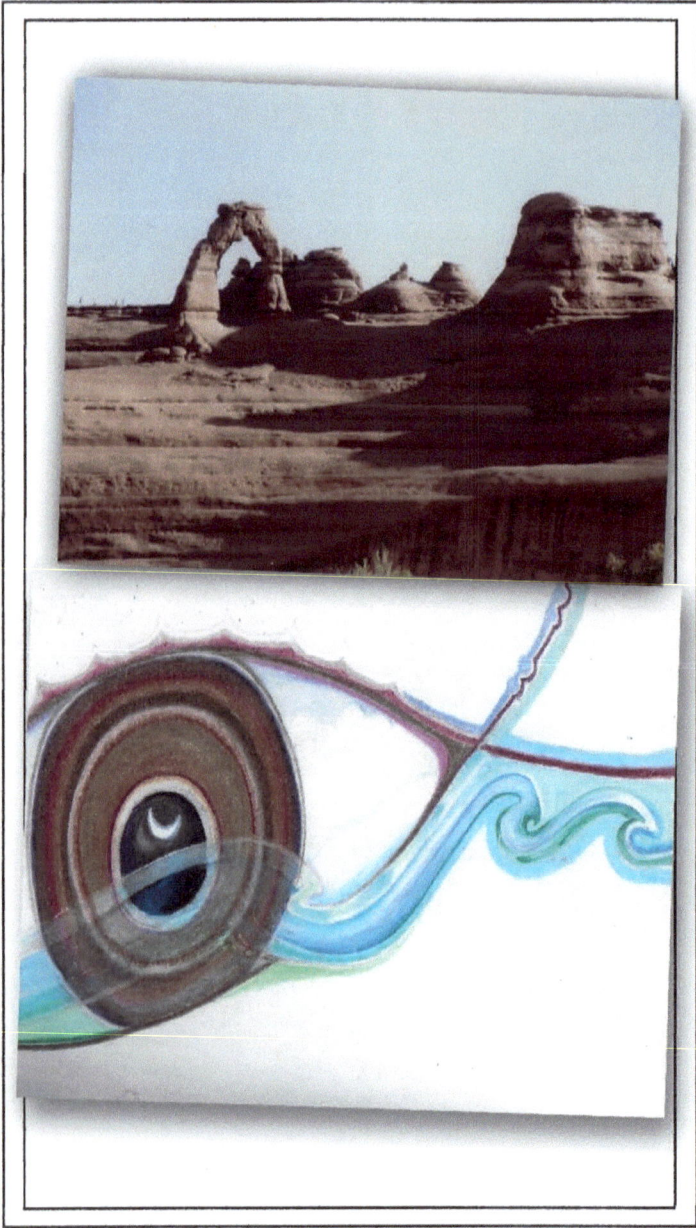

1000 BCE to 000 CE
Common Era

Leucippus posits the atom.
Roman Leptis Magna is founded.
Yu Sze is the Imperial Chinese Jester.
Democritus advocates inductive reasoning.
We know of Mozi, and the School of Names.
Theatre with Thespis in Greece; and then in Rome,
Susarin bands of comedians herald Comedia dell'arte.
Humans live in Athens, Thebes, Sparta, and Nubian Egypt.
Ashurbanipal has a 20,000-tablet library at Nineveh.
Chavin Peruvians, and Paracas develop a culture
of South American farming communities.
We hear of Saul, David, and Solomon,
a Great Temple in Jerusalem:
first Hebrew inscriptions
and Judaic Literature;
first vowel alphabets;
the Gezer calendar,
and metal coins.
Here are Chou China,
Aeschylus, Heraclitus, and
Pythagorean mystical mathematics.
There are the Parthenon, democracy,
Jainism, and Homer with
The Iliad and *The Odyssey.*
In the Valley of the Kings,
is the tomb of Tutankhamun.
In Assyria is a Palace of Sargon II,
and trumpets are being made of bronze.
Terpander completes the musical octave.
Rome is enlarged, and we see Kushite Nubia.
We assemble seven wonders of the world:
Statue and Temple of Zeus at Olympia,
Pharaoh's Lighthouse at Alexandria,
the Mausoleum at Hallicarnassus,
Gardens within Babylon Hang,
Diana's Temple is at Ephesus,
pyramids are in Egypt, and
at Rhodes is a Colossus.

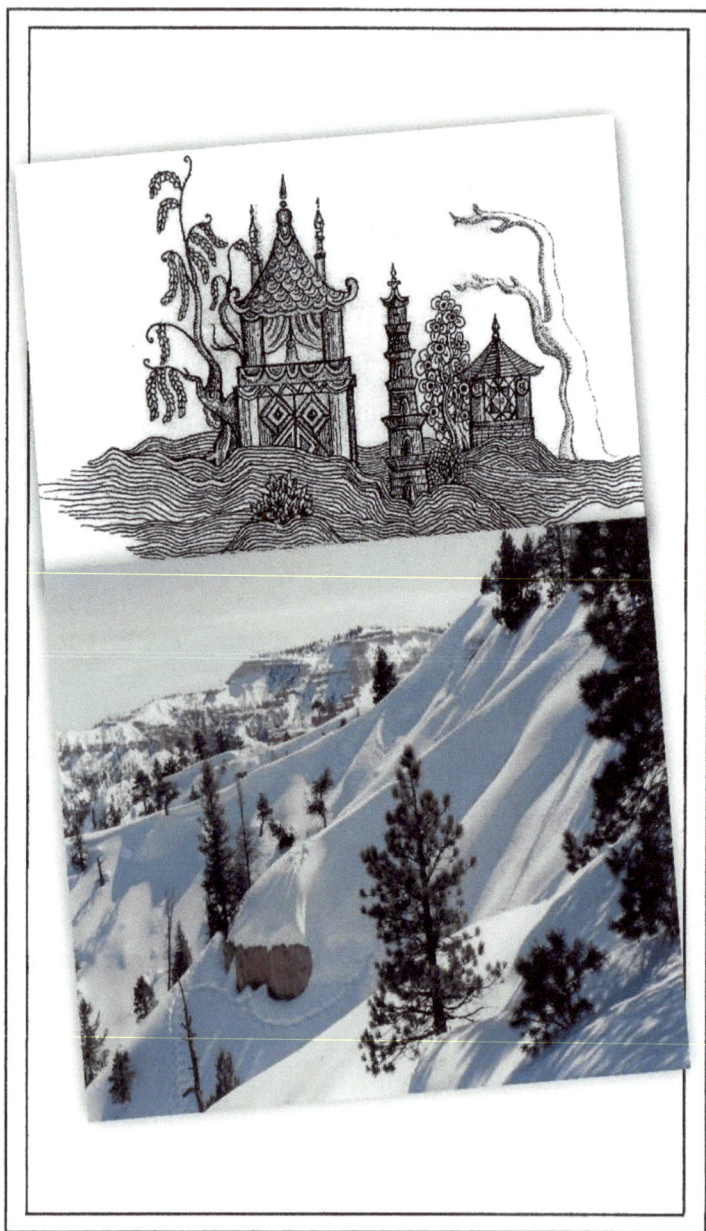

We engage war in Peloponnese.
Transport has the first ships
with double banks of oars,
cotton as a trade crop, &
extensive mining, and
iron replaces copper.
People enjoy using
fluked metal anchors,
spoked wheel chariots,
timber frame buildings,
hoists, pulleys, hydraulics,
the door key, and the lathe.
The Etruscans flourish.
The Mahabarata, and
The Upanishads arrive.
The Rig Veda is completed.
Casts are established in India with
Magadha, Chandragupta, and Ashoka.
Greek civilization, and theatre develop.
Saka Scythians are at Steppes of Eurasia.
Tamil remains our oldest written language.
Maurya gathers together Iron-age India.
Also comes to the earth new realities
beckoned by: Lao Tsu, as in the Tao,
Kung Fu Tsu - Confucian - mind,
Sidartha Gautama - the Buddha,
Yoga Sutras and Yogi Mahavira.
Begins the Buddhist calendar.
Beijing becomes capital of an
ancient Middle Kingdom.
Judah and Israel separate.
See Yuezhi, and Bactria.
Nebuchadnezzar is King.
Chinese states are at war.
We have timber buildings
with footings made of stone.
Greek architecture develops with
the Erechtheion, and Propylaea
entry into the Acropolis.

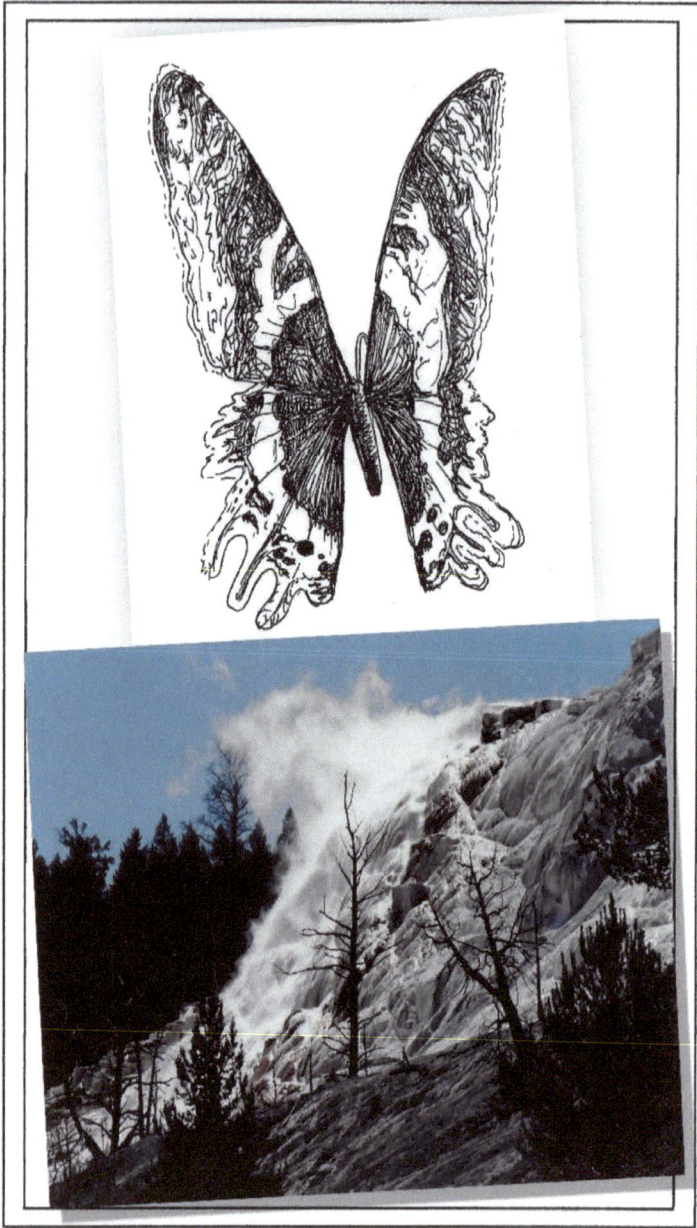

1000 BCE to 000 CE (3)

Carthage is founded.
There are astronomical observations.
Our first archaeologist is Nabonidus.
We have an agricultural calendar, and
Yu Hsi describes precession of the equinoxes.
There are Nok Nigeria, appearance of maize, and
the Amun, Sun, Lion, and Isis temples at Meroe.
We lived as Hopewell mound builders and
Marpole peoples in North America;
Villanovan Tuscany is established,
while elsewhere we become:
Nazca Peruvians, Zapotecs,
Myans, Andean cultures,
Teotihuacán Mexicans,
Saladero Venezuelans.
Somewhere in here are
legendary beginnings of
Japan as Shinto emerges.
Etruscans build the Temple
of Jupiter Optimus Maximus.
Achaemenid Column Architecture
arrives along with Empire in Persia.
Epicurus proposes direct observation
and deduction in search of truth as
atomism is studied by the Greeks,
and there is rusticated masonry.
Herophilos Erasistratus of Chios
runs medical research experiments.
Begins 2,200 years of feudal society.

1000 BCE to 000 CE (4)

We express ourselves as
Alexander the Great, & Hannibal.
Eratosthenes grasps calculation of
the diameter of our small planet.
We see the first Olympic games.
Bronze dawns in Nam Viet,
as Korean records emerge.
Babylonians capture Jews,
and there are Punic Wars.
Obelisks are built to Heliopolis
in Lantern, & as Cleopatra's Needle.
Baths of Diocletian are the largest ever.
Ruwanveliseya stupa reaches 300 feet.
Chinese people invent paper,
compass, and cross-bow,
with the Zhou Empire.
Yayoi dominates Japan.
There is extensive tunneling.
Urban architecture produces
assembly building, and stadiums.
Media becomes Parthia & becomes Iran.
Heracleion prospers; then lost and found.
Corinthian columns appear, and there are
inventions: roller bearing carts, silverware,
decimals, piston bellows, cast iron in China.
Nyaya, Vaisesika, and Buddhist forms appear.
Pons fabricius footbridge still crosses the Tiber.
Rome expands with: the Temple of Foruna Virilis,
a Theater of Marcellus, and the temple of Hercules
Circus Maximus, Imperial Fora, Forum of Augustus.
Mayans build structures at Uaxactun and Lamanai.

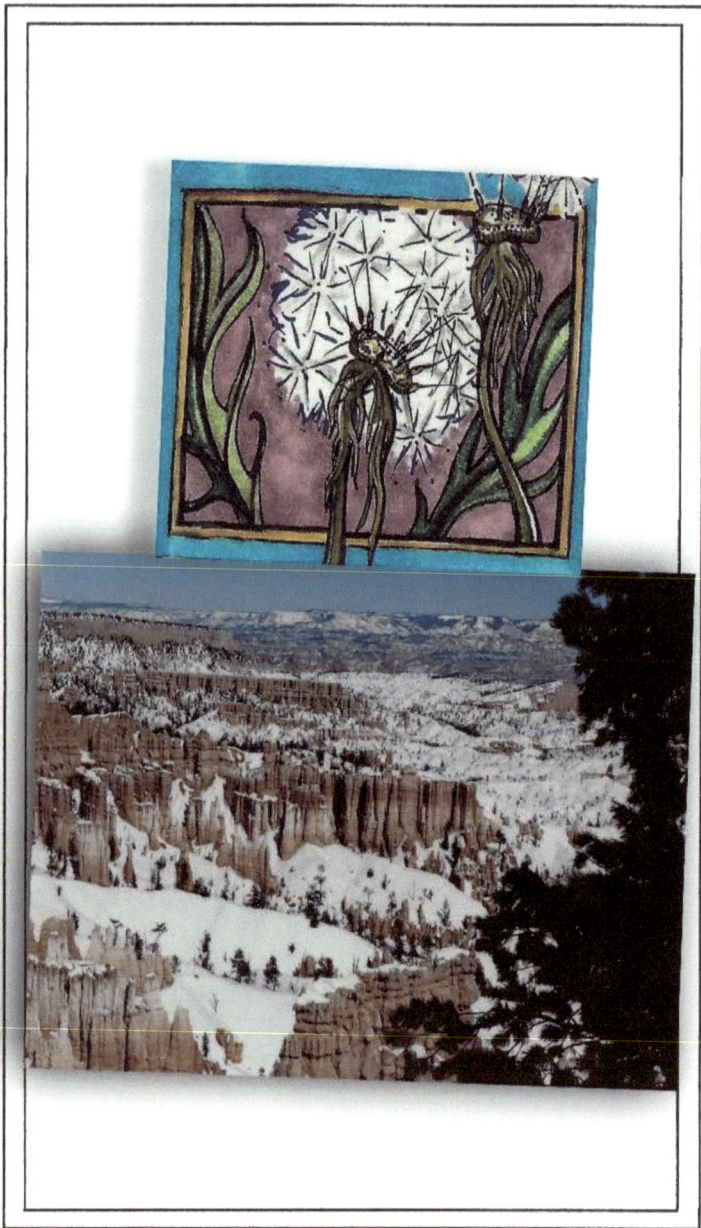

1000 BCE to 000 CE ₍₅₎

There are gymnasiums, and a Theatre Epidaurus.
Romans build basilica and amphitheaters,
Pompeii, triumphal arches town gates,
villas, aqueducts and bridges.

We have Doric Temples built to honor
Neptune, Hephaestus, Hera, Asklepios,
Samos, Sounion, Apollo, and Poseidon.
Humans grow: Euclid, Plato, Socrates,
Aristotle, Aristophanes, Agnodice.
Euripides, Archimedes, Thales,
Anaxagoras, and Diogenes.
Geometry is used along
with large numbers.

Epicurus produces
the first map of a known world.
There is a keystone tunnel vault.
The chisel is made multi-toothed.
Aristarchus maintains that
the earth revolves
around the sun.

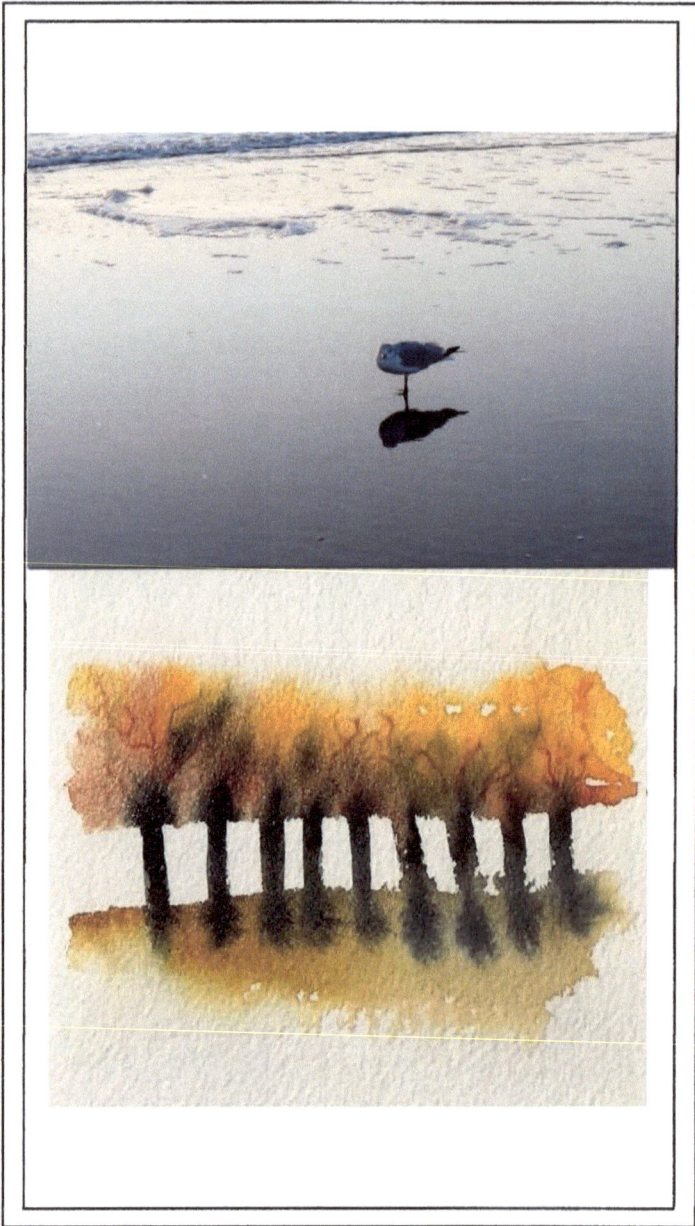

1000 BCE to 000 CE (6)

.

We hear of an 'orchestra',
then a kettle drum; & know
first keyboard instruments,
A seven-note scale appears, and
there is the hydraulis. We receive
Bhagavad Gita, and Ramayana epics.
People live as Aesop, Zoroaster, and
Sappho, and Sophocles, & we
have Draco's laws on homicide.
Society has Caesar Augustus,
Virgil, Ovid, Judas Maccabus,
Cicero, and Herod the Great.
Venus de Milo is created.
Julius Caesar adopts a
calendar of 365.25 days.
We enter ages of palaces and fortresses.
There is the Great Sanchi Stupa in India,
and Chavin Pyramids of the Sun and Moon.
We have Sunga India, Wu of Zhou, and Quin China.
Effective drainage is installed by Agora of Athens.
Eclipse of the sun is predicted for the first time.
In France the Maison Carree is designed, then
to inspire Thomas Jefferson 1700 years after.
There are Pharisees, Sadduces, and Essenes.
Highly centralized bureaucracy expands.
Christ is born of the House of David.
Eratosthenes - fathers geography.
The World population is
200 Million.

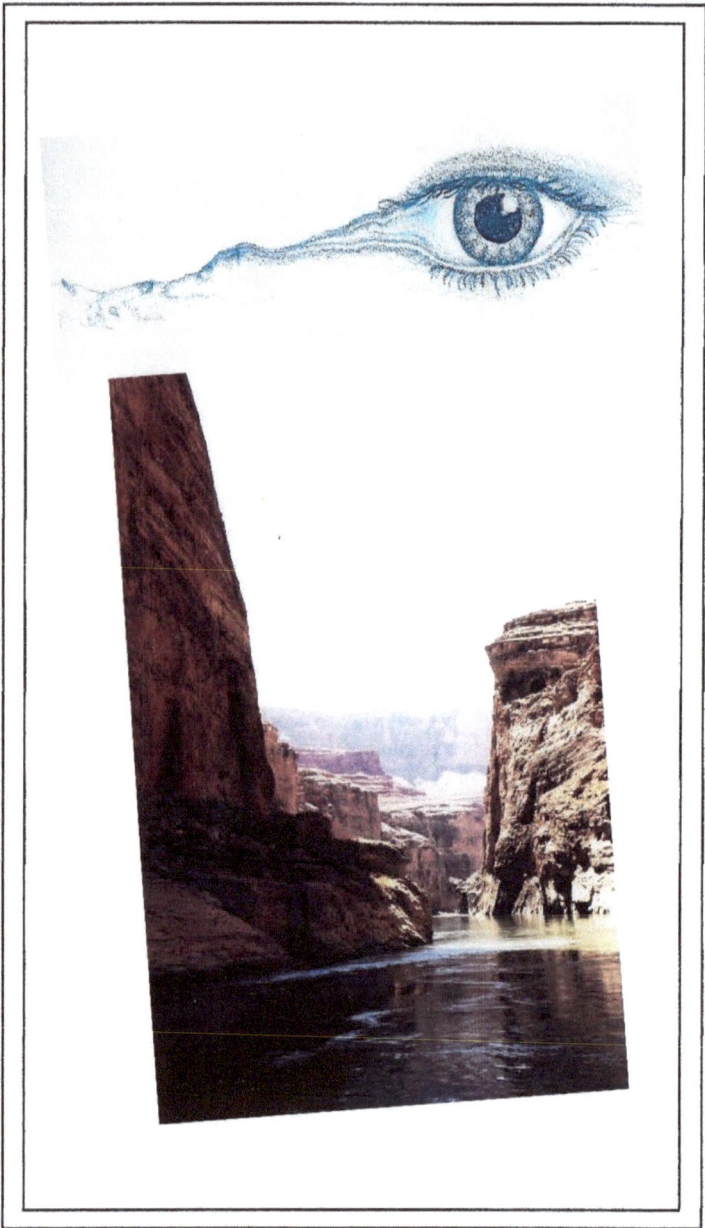

000 to 200 CE

With a new millennium:
Gnosticism, Manichaeanism,
Montanism, Mithraism, Stoicism,
Pontias Pilot, Nero, and Plutarch.
The Roman Empire expands to the
Pont du Gard aqueduct of France.
See the largest vaulted interior,
until the 15th century;
The Pantheon;
and Bath, and
Hadrian's wall.
Umayyade, Samanid,
and Chaznavid develop India.
Saul of Tarsus seeds Christianity.
A Gospel is separated from apocrypha.
St. Peter is designated first of the Popes.
Marcus Aurelius speaks to us, there are:
Roman columns, surgical instruments,
the Colosseum, Flavian's Amphitheater.
The first non-Euclidian geometry appears.
We learn from the Sanskrit poet Asvaghosa.
The temple at Yeha presages Axum Ethiopia.
Arab civilization emerges as does Satrap India.
Sanskrit emerges, and the Kamasutra is begun.
We see the completion of Trajan's Forum by
Apollodorus of Damascus, and the Temple
of the Divine Trajan, by Apollodorus.
Avicenna criticizes Aristotle.
Alhazen composes *Book of Optics.*
Han China, and the abacus is in use.
Izapa Mexicans and Mayans appear.
We have concave & convex mirrors.
Mount Vesuvius captures Pompeii forever.
The second Jewish Temple is destroyed
resulting in dispersion of the Hebrews.

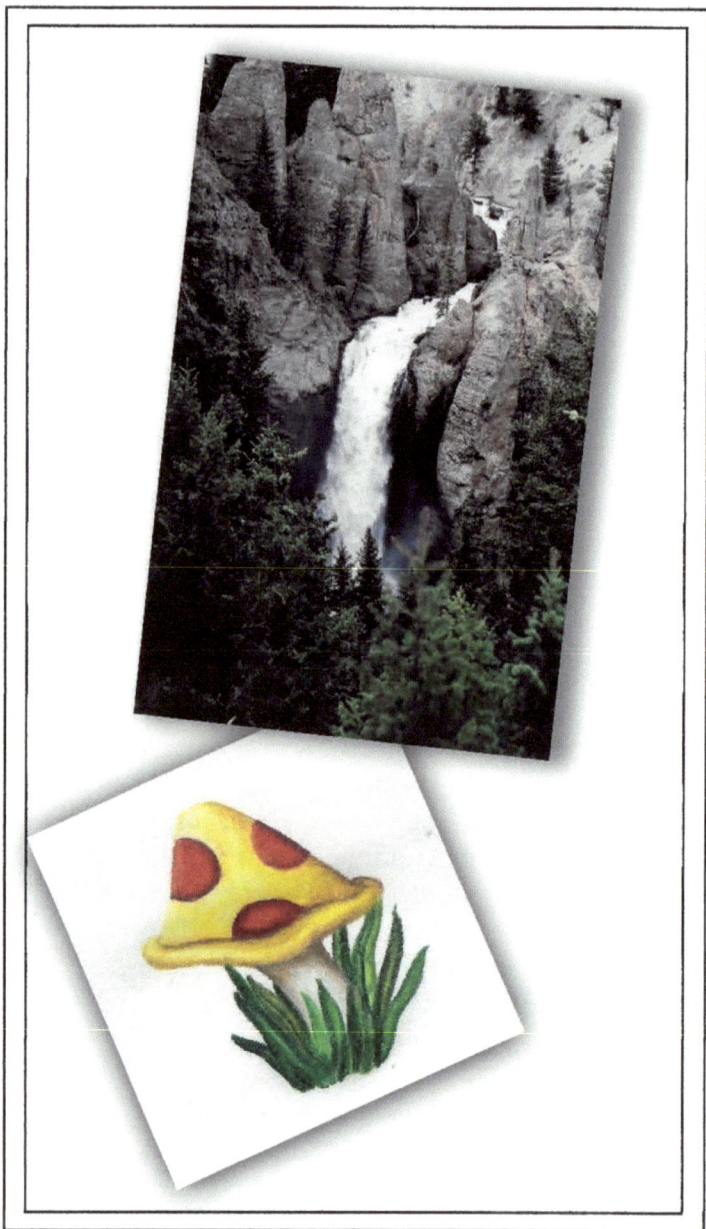

000 to 200 CE (2)

Sri Lanka supports a Lambakanna Dynasty.
Alphabetics carries language to the next levels.
Hipparchus fancies astronomy and Geography.
Heron of Alexandria is the great experimenter.
Arab civilization emerges, as does Satrap India.
Khmer, and Funan precede, Viet Nam,
Cambodia, Thailand, and Myanmar.
We learn from the poet Asvaghosa.
Paper begins to record our story.
Cultures grow around the globe.
Our first science fiction fantasy
is *The True History*, written by Lucian.
A first non-Euclidian geometry appears.
More new kingdoms and empires in India:
Pallavas, Kalabhras, Nanda, and Kushan nomads.
We grow as Lâm Ấp in Viet Nam, and Shu Han,
Cao Wei, Dong Wu, Xiongnu are in China, and
Black Sea Greutungi arrive before Ostrogoths.
The Langkasuka were on Sumatra, and Borneo.
Galen of Pergamum produced Medical texts.
In Southeast Asia are the Pyu Cities.
Cements supply our foundations.
Boadicea is Iceni warrior queen.
The Champa are in Indochina.
Goths migrate, and we see
the Pyramid of the Sun.
The abacus is in use.
We also have concave and convex mirrors,
a wheelbarrow, and the Chinese Xither.
Mount Vesuvius preserves Pompeii.
Ptolomy's astronomy redefines a
place in the heavens, and
there were Skeptics, and
the world population
comes to about
300 Million.

200 to 400 CE

The Han dynasty falls and
Ch'in is in China finishing
a great wall, and destroying
all but a very small portion of
Chinese literature. Zero is first
used as a cypher. Pi is decided to
be equal to 3.1547.
We see the first Christian monastery.
There are palaces and garden pavilions.
Tumulus rules the Japanese culture;
the Axum Kingdom matures, and
Constantine is in Rome, then
Constantinople is founded.
St. Augustine is born.
Mons Vaticanus is leveled to allow
the building of the Basilica of St. Peter.
Jetavana stupa in Sri Lanka reaches 400 feet.
Hypatia of Alexandria measures and seeks.
Diophantus of Alexandria authors algebra.
Churches, commemorative structures;
Vakatakas, Kadambas, Kamrupa.
More Indian Kingdoms develop.
Covered cemeteries appear.
We witness Sassanid Persia,
emergence of Gupta India,
and written records come
with the uniting of Japan.
The science of breeding,
and raising horses matures.
Classical Sanskrit theatre appears.
St. Marcella founds Monasticism.
Symbols produce Greek algebra,
Germanic runes appear, and
invasions of Europe begin.
The Hawaiian Islands are
peopled by Polynesians,
Myans are at Palenque.
The Anasazi develop.

400 to 600 CE

In a flash of time
a Roman Empire falls.
The Arthurian stories appear,
ending at Avalon-Glastonbury.
The Franks and Burgundians settle.
Europe is swamped into darkness by
Huns, Goths, Visigoths, and Vandals.
Mausolea and baptisteries are built.
Aspasia consorts Pericles in Athens.
The Anglo-Saxon culture emerges.
Sun Ken Palace is in Istanbul.
Byzantine Empire expands.
Empress Theodora reigns.
Slavic cultures develop.
University is founded
at Constantinople.
Chenla people settle
between Funan and Khmer.
Anasazi are in Horseshoe Canyon.
Srivijaya begin 600 years in Indonesia.
Math and astronomy gain ground
with Aryabhata, Thales of Miletus
and Brahmagupta.
Asuka Japanese culture grows
with building of Shinto shrines.
Tiflis in Georgia is founded, and
St. Augustine of Hippo writes
The City of God.

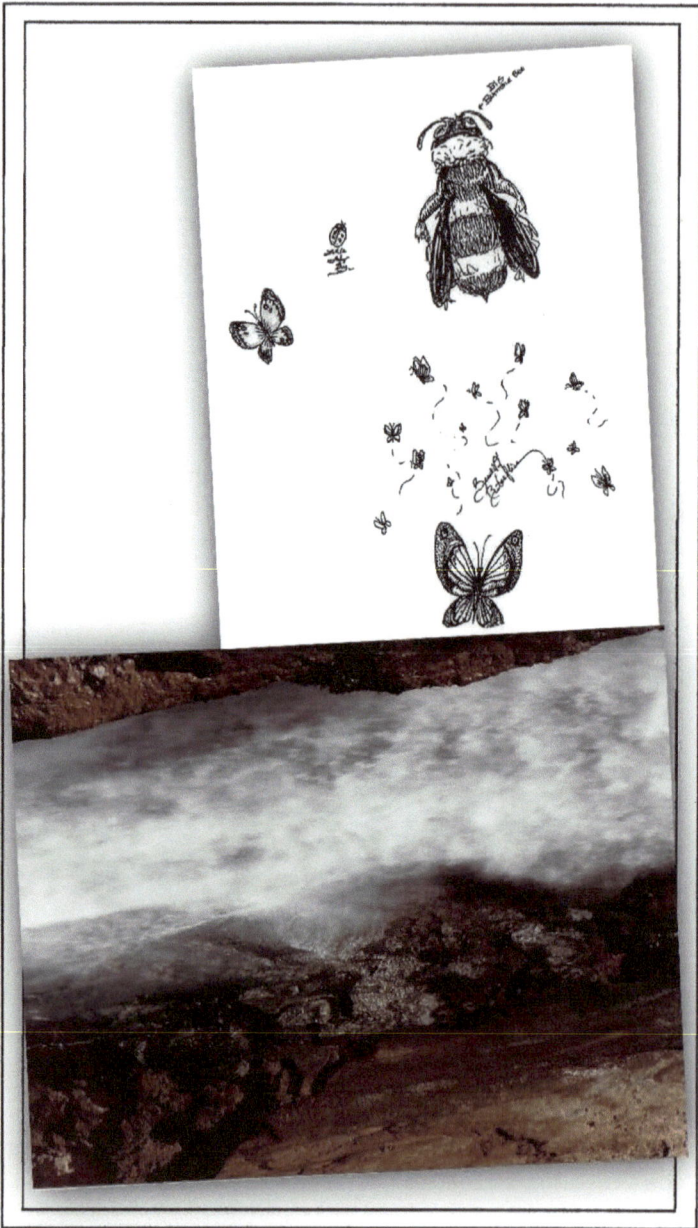

400 to 600 CE (2)

Muhammed arrives.
The Islamic calendar emerges.
Musical letter notation appears.
The House of the Prophet inspires
beginnings of Islamic architecture.
Santa Sophia is in Constantinople.
The earth experiences Sui China,
as Japanese writing develops.
The Empire of Ghana, and
the Marimba Bantu
culture appears.
China is united.
St. Patrick is in Ireland,
Vedisam, and ragas develop.
Theodora is Byzantine Empress.
We have Justinians, Benedictines.
Buddhist sacred literature develops.
The Jewish Haggadah text advances.
Humans mature the Zapotec culture,
expanded Anasazi Pueblo culture, and
we know of bows and arrows in North
America, and Gregorian chants appear,
as pre-Incans, and paleontology develop.
Justinian's Hagia Sophia Church dominates.
New knowledge by Anthemius and Isodorus.
Germania is occupied by Gallæcians, Gepids,
Huns, Goths, Jutes, and Frisians.
Ostrogoths are in Italy.

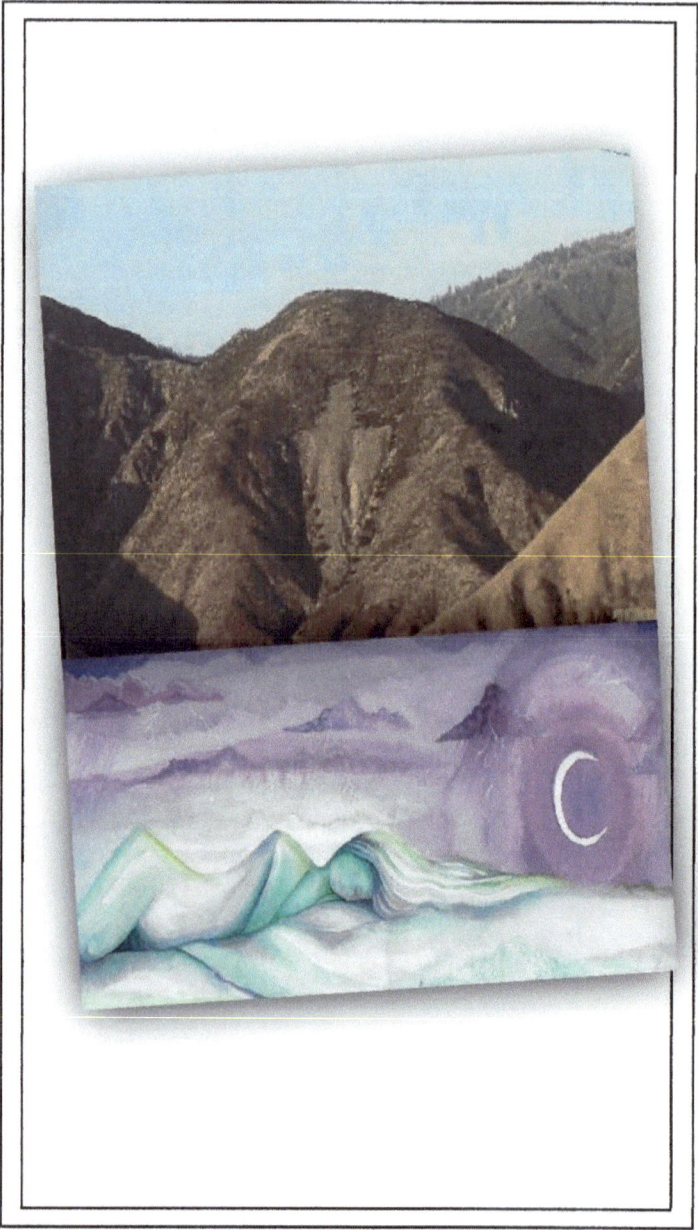

600 to 800

Tang is in china.
Muhammed leaves.
A Talmud is complete.
Myans build extraordinary
structures at Xuphil and Tikal.
Anji Bridge is built in Zhaoxian.
Then, wooden kodo and pagoda at
Horyuji, Japan, survives until today.
Derinkuyu, underground, is in Turkey.
The Teotihuacán city culture develops.
Slavic-Turkish-Bulgarian Empire grows.
Windmills appear, and Chess is invented.
There is the first Potala Palace in Lhasa.
The Bulgars commission cathedrals.
The Borobudur Temple is in Java.
The Persians expand an empire.
Greek Language replaces Latin.
There are gridiron plan cities.
Traveling circuses appear.
Theatre appears in China.
Medieval theatre appears
at Tiahuanaco, and Huari.
Architecture calls itself Romanesque,
with cathedral, baptistery and tower,
doorways, nave piers, asps, porches,
facade, fontevault, and cloisters.
Calculations pave the way with
Jābir ibn Hayyān; Al-khwarizmi.
The culture of the Celts matures in
Northern Europe and Britain, and
The Book of Psalms appears in Anglo-Saxon.
Cahokia Mounds begin 800 years in Mississippi.
We know the Venerable Bede and Beowulf,
bronze bells, organ pipes,
and Coptic Christians.

600 to 800 (2)

We know *The Qur'an*,
the Dome of the Rock,
and The Arabian Nights.
Baghdad is founded as is
the Academy of Science.
Islam inspires and expands.
Arab influence grows as a Great
Mosque is constructed in Damascus,
We see Charlemagne, Aachen Cathedral,
Li Po, Wang Wei, and iconoclasm.
Mayans Temple the Giant Jaguar.
Ummayad and Abbasid Caliphate
reigns over all of Islam.
There were T'ang China,
with Civil Service tests,
invention of gunpowder,
removal of cataracts, and
Gurjara-Prathihara India;
Vikings sail across oceans.
Nara Japan, block printing;
the Khmer Empire expands.
Shi'ites, Sunni, Khawarij, and
Urban South America develops.
Heian influences are in Japan, and
there are Tabot'ap, and Sokkat'ap.
Mississippians appear.
Kanem-Bornu emerge.
Sufi Muslims develop.
Pagodas in Pulguska.
Myans flourish.

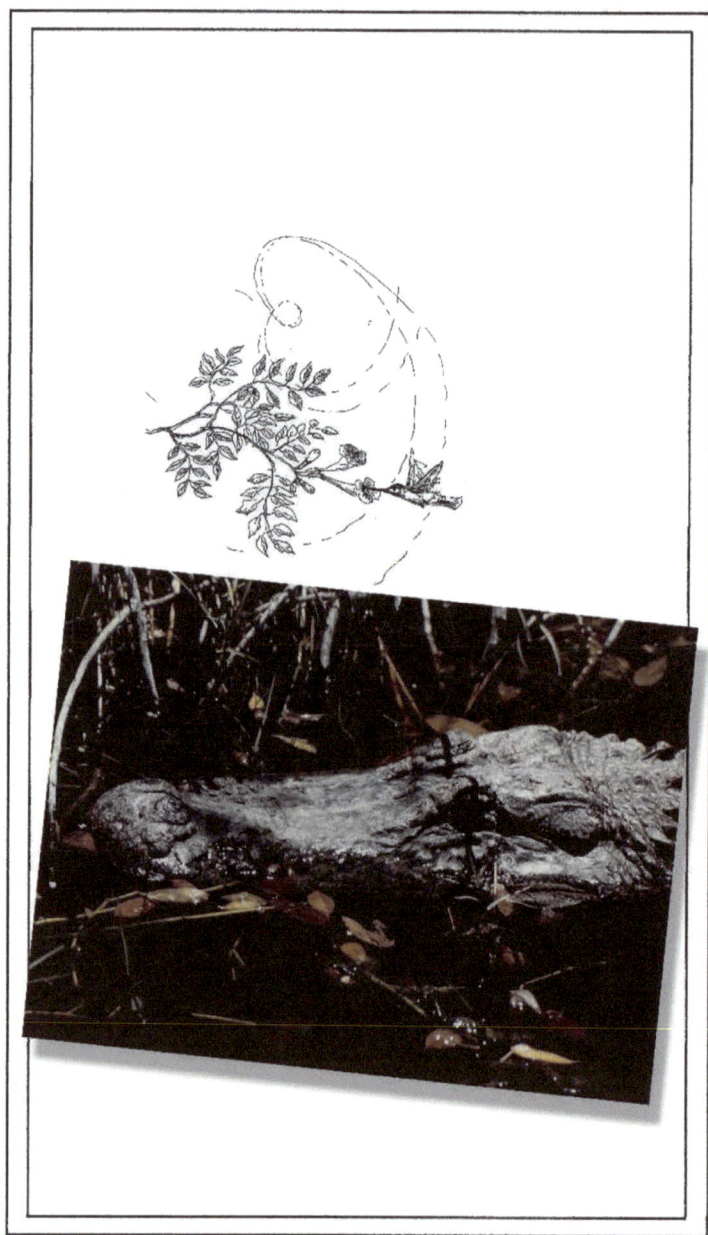

800 to 1000

We conceive an
Arabic alphabet
with numerals.
The Ottoman empire extends.
Turkish India develops, and Cairo is Founded.
In Nigeria, subterranean Igbo-Ukwu tombs.
There is the Hindu rock cut Kailasa Temple.
Fatimid Caliphate lasts three centuries.
In St. Gall is the Ideal monastery plan.
The Cordoba Mosque has been built;
also the Malwiya at Samarra, and
The Great Mosque at Qairouan.
A University of al-Qarawiyyin
is founded in Fez, Morocco.
There are Ashi Japanese,
Genji tales from Japan,
Sun's Dynasty, and
the Scandinavians.
The Magyars grow.
Norway is founded,
People, and cultures
flourish in the old world.
Icelandic culture develops.
Idrisid people hold West Africa.
There are pilgrimage churches in
Italy, France, Britain, Scandinavia.
Saxons, and Danes are in England.
Spain, Portugal and the Holy lands.
The Thaton Mon kingdoms begin a
millennium rule of lower Burma,
Ameer, Khitan, and Song.

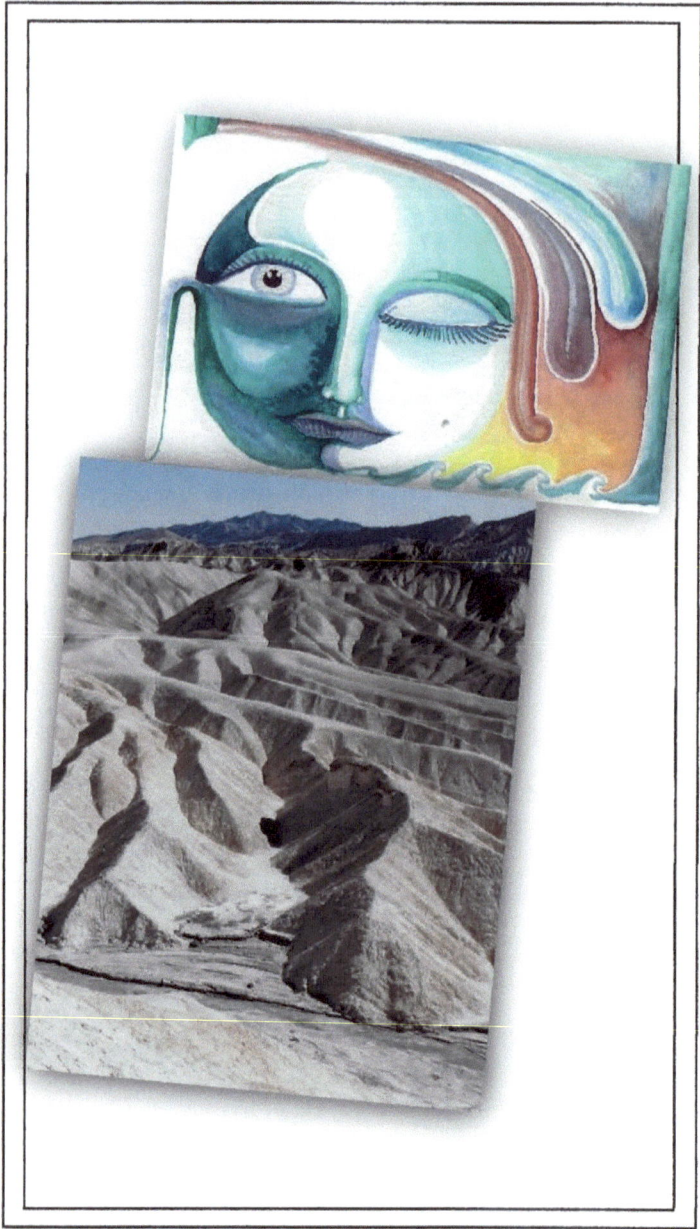

800 to 1000 (2)

A Holy Roman Empire is founded and
Christianity expands its influence.
Vikings invade Europe.
Gernrode Abby has
a triforium gallery;
alternating supports.
Sa'adia ben Joseph founds
a Jewish Academy in Babylon.
The Principality of Russia is founded.
Ibn Sina writes of medicine and philosophy.
The Polish State is formed, Bohemia emerges,
the Greek Orthodox Church is founded,
and there are Toltec Mexicans, as
Hopewell native Americans
etch designs with acid,
and Burma takes shape.
In China there are optical lenses.
Guido of Arezzo confirms musical notation,
and Fan Kuan paints mountain landscapes.
Along with Ecclesiastical Architecture,
we see the mechanical clock, and
the astrolabe.

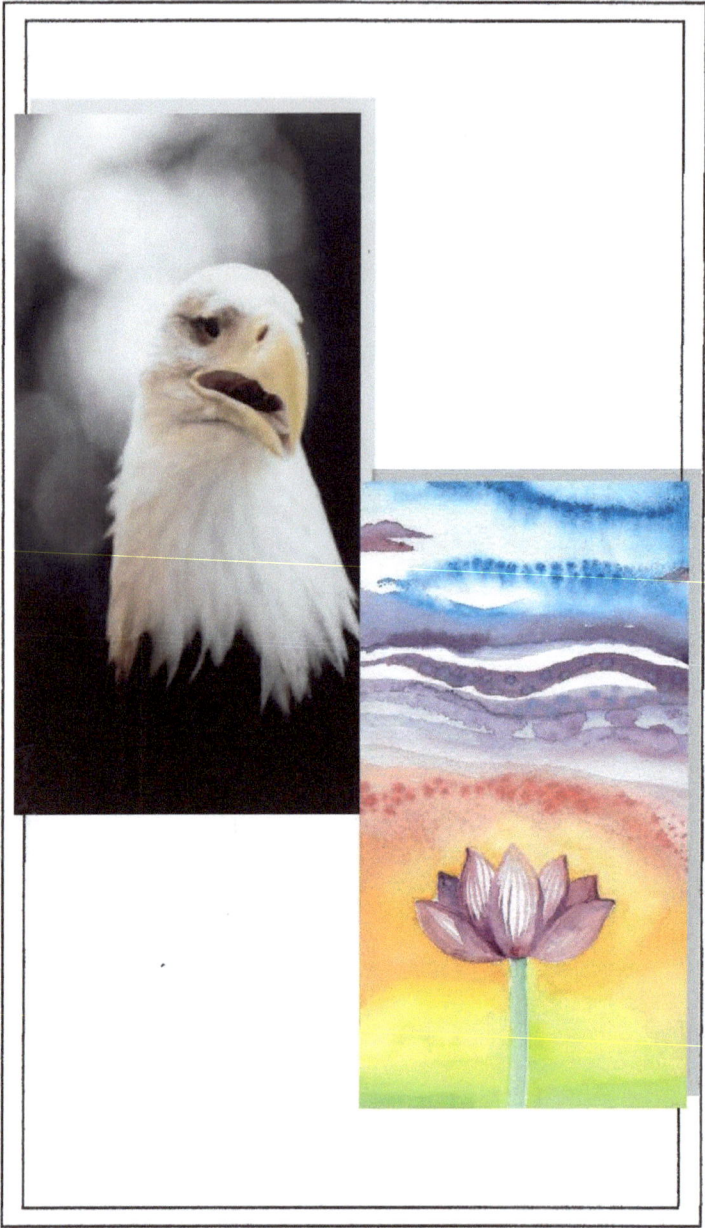

1000 to 1200

Brings the Sufi Mystic Ghazil,
Choila India, Seljuks, and Korro Nigeria.
Jains carve a Dilwarra Temple of marble.
The Monks Mound at Cahokia is the
largest single ceremonial building
of pre-colonial North America.
A Great Temple is at Tanjore.
Mali West Africa emerges,
and Leif Erickson arrives
on the American Coast.
William the Conqueror
founds Norman England
with a Battle at Hastings in 1066.
Buddhists build Phoenix Hall at Byodo'in.
The Benedictines have Maria Laach Abbey,
Westminster Abbey, and a Doomsday Book.
Sana'a is the most ancient site of human habitation.
Castles crown Restormel, Orford, and Hedingham.
San Miniato al Monte uses an Early Christian plan.
Sexpartite vaulting used in Abbaye-aux-Hommes,
Liao China gives us Kumsansa Temple in Kimche.
The University is founded in Bologna.
There is Independence for Portugal.
New methods of science spawn.
Al-Biruni designs a pin-hole camera.
Adelard of Bath brings numerals to Europe.
Ibn ali enhances a method of science even as
Robert Grossetese extends it to England.
Maimonides completes
The Mishmah Torah.
Kabalism emerges.
Murasaki Shikibu
composes the first novel.
Ibn Rushd translates Aristotle.

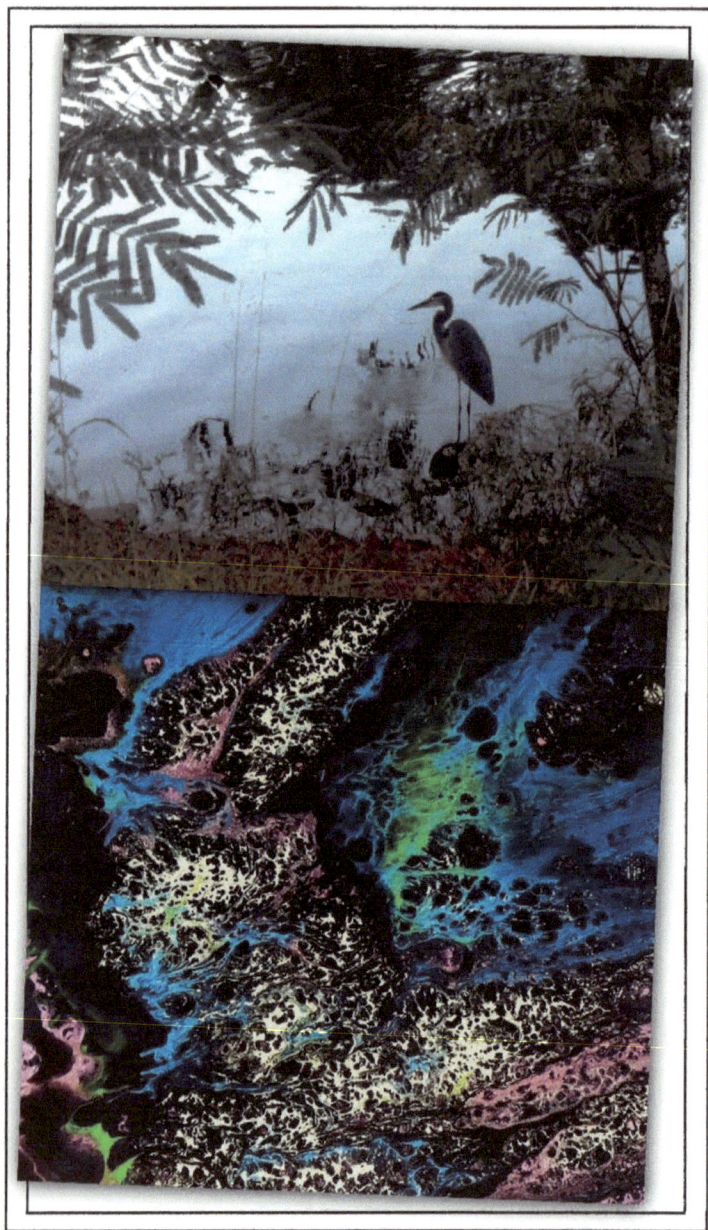

1000 to 1200 (2)

Sima Jin Dynasty followed by Mongolians.
Minowara Japan blossoms, Judo is born,
and in theatre, Noh drama emerges.
The Chinese record a Supernova.
There are the Knights Templar,
the first of nine Crusades, and
there is Eleanor of Aquetaine.
Zen Buddhism emerges, and
Zhu Xi restores Confucius.
Ghenghis Khan appears.
Moscow is founded and
the Georgian Queen Tamar reigns.
Kievan Russia knows development
of the Eastern an Orthodox church.
In Europe a royal family emerges.
In England are
the Plantagenets.
Universities are founded at
Oxford and Cambridge.
Thomas á Becket is
the Archbishop
of Canterbury.
Alcohol is distilled.
Innocent III is Pope.
Avignon Bridge is built, and
Old London Bridge is constructed.

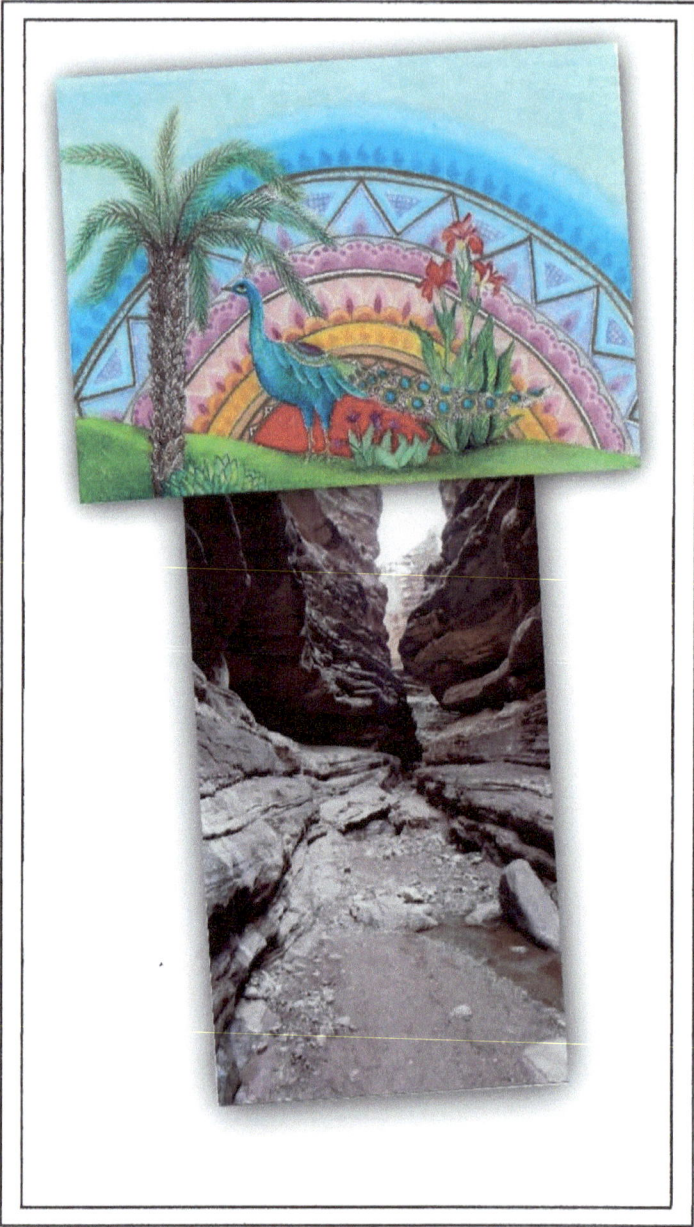

1000 to 1200 (3)

The second Bulgar Empire emerges.
Shijia Pagoda is in Shanxi province.
In Burma there is the glorious Ananda Temple.
In Cambodia the Angkor Vat Temple is completed.
Constantine's Church of the Holy Sepulchre is expanded.
There are minarets at Ghurid and Bokhara.
Christian Spain expands, Guilds develop,
Abbott Suger connects theology to light.
The Abbey Church of St. Dennis is built.
Gothic Architecture spills forth upon
the earth and the people with high
nave vaulting at St. Ambrogio, and
domes, and flying buttresses, and
also 35 different kinds of arches.
A Song compass points the way.
Borgund Church graces Norway.
Stained glass windows abound.
Berber North Africa prospers.
The Mossi Kingdom appears.
In a Cathedral is founded
Paris University.
Al-Biruni designs a pin-hole camera.
Adelard of Bath brings numerals to Europe.
Ibn al-Haytham creates a method of science.
Robert Grossetese founds
Franciscan science.
We see the development of
the Swahili language, Ife Nigeria,
the Kamakura Ashikaga Shoganate, and
Nichiren Buddhists, as Zen arrives in Japan.
In Ghana, the Sosso, Songhai, and Ashanti
extend their kingdoms another 500 years.

1200 to 1400

The Ottoman Turks mature, and
Arabic numerals arrive in Europe.
The Magna Carta is signed in 1215.
Observatories are
in the Arabic world.
Jalal Ad-Din Ar-Rumi
is the first whirling dervish.
The Shah-i-Zindeh burial ground
at Samarkand stands as necropolis.
Yuan names China to last 400 years.
Crusaders build Krak of the Knights.
We build mechanical steel crossbows,
forged iron guns, and the Sitar appears.
Abbeys lead the way toward cathedrals.
The Mudejar build La Lugareja, Arevado.
Reimes and Laon Cathedrals rise,
England's early entries are
Salisbury Cathedral; and
Notre Dame Cathedral
speaks the Gothic ideal.
and Old St. Paul's Cathedral is begun.
Hildegarde of Bingen establishes science.
Kamal al-Din al-Farisi expands optic vision.
Frescoes by Giotto deify St. Francis at Assisi.
Florence outgrows the Palace of the Podesta.
It is to be replaced by the Palazzo Vecchio.
Gambio designs the Florence Cathedral.
The collapse of the Beauvais Cathedral
limits the height of the Gothic dream.
St. John Aleitourgetos is in Bulgaris;
Church of the Intercession in Russia.
Gaddi designs Ponte Vecchio.

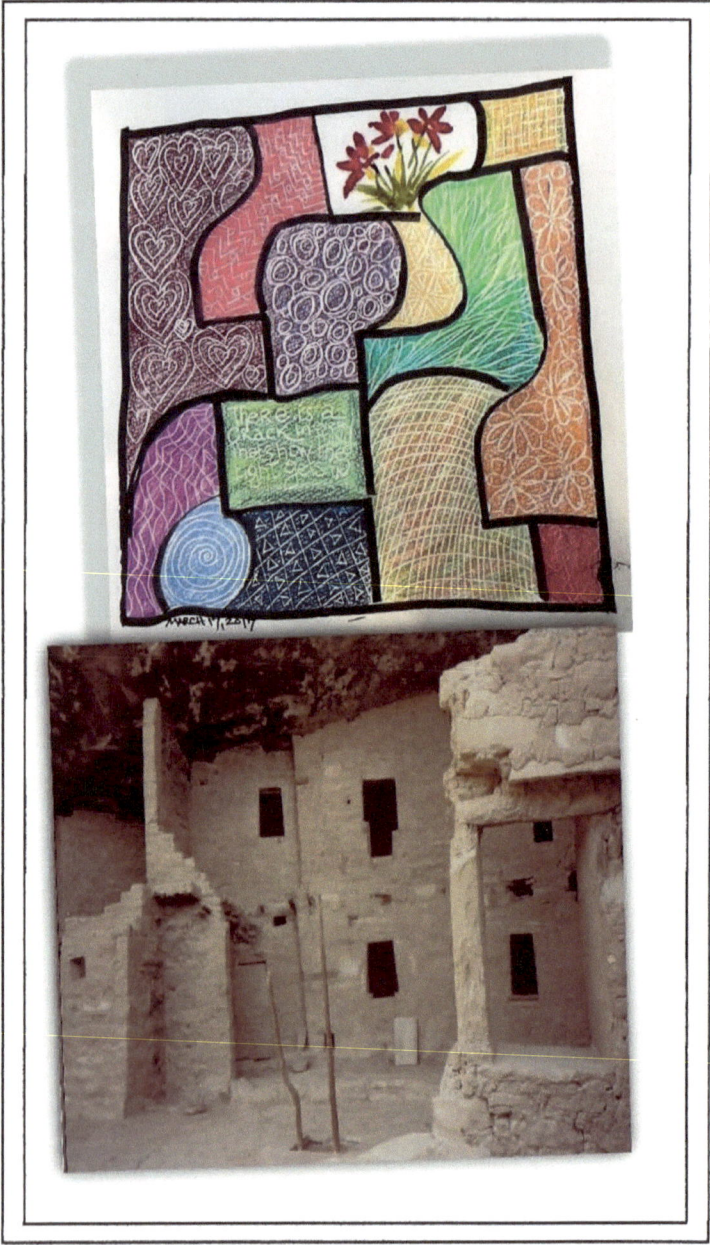

1200 to 1400 (2)

We find ourselves influenced:
Saint Thomas Aquinas,
William of Ockham,
The Society of Jesus,
Fibonacci, Boccaccio, and
Dominicans, and Franciscans.
Mongols begin invasions of Europe.

The Alhambra
Muslim Palace, beckons from Spain.
Pisano sculpts a facade on Siena Cathedral.
Ibn Battuta travels the Muslim world,
and Ibn Khaldun writes its history.
First English plays are presented.
The final crusade is launched.
The Sorbonne is founded.
Chaco Canyon culture is
in America's Southwest.

Moscow matures,
and Tenochtitlan is founded.
Humans are using Gold currency,
double entry bookkeeping, and the
Hanseatic League for trade develops.
Perhaps half the European population
is taken by The Bubonic Plague.
German drama develops.

Comes a 'Hundred Years War'
along with a precursor to
the blast furnace;
the stuckofen.
We have linen clothing,
lock gates in Dutch canals,
spring wheels, & reading glasses.

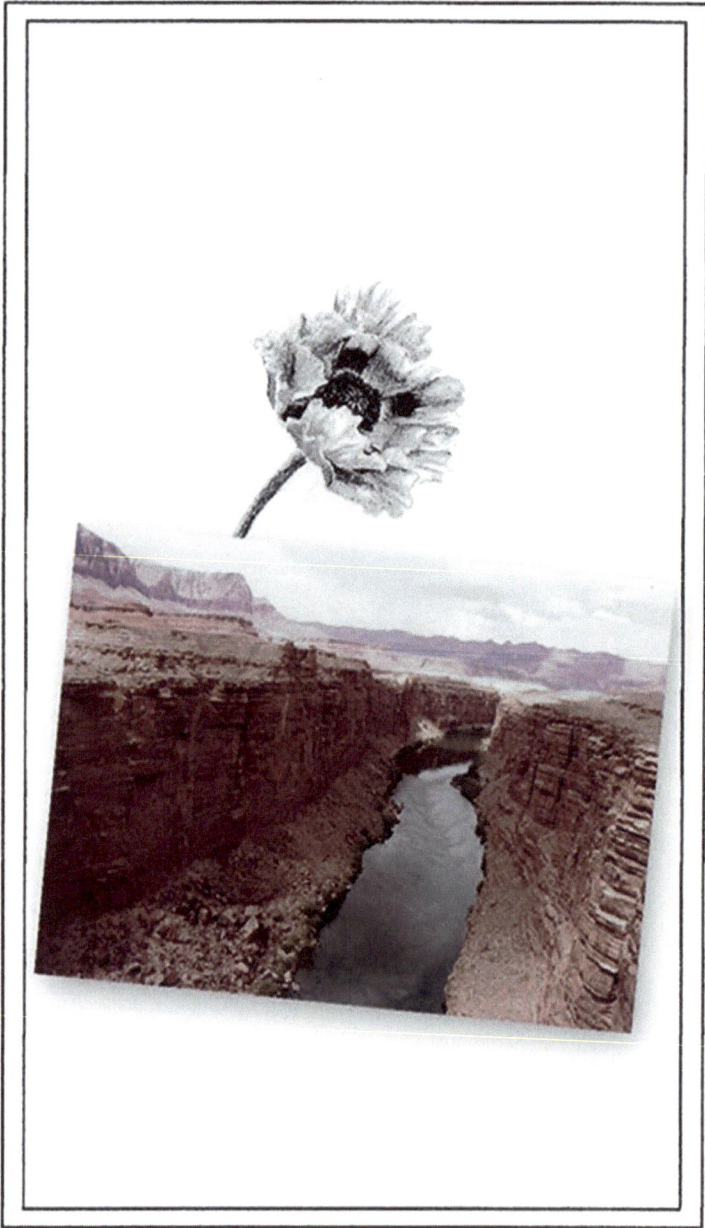

1200 to 1400 (3)

The Gračanica Church is built.
We hear from Roger Bacon, Dante,
Chaucer, Kublai Khan, and Marco Polo,
as Jews are expelled from England, and France.
There is a beginning of the Vijayanagar Dynasty,
the last chapter in a history of independent china.
We begin the experience of a 450-year mini ice age.
Petronilla de Meath is burned for a witch.
The Jains are building the Palitana.
Heidelberg University is founded.
Fan vaults are introduced at
a cloister in Gloucester.
A madrigal appears, and
the Hapsburgs are in Austria.
The Kremlin is first mentioned.

In North America
are Athabascans; and
the Iroquois are living by
The Great Laws of Peace.
Mississippian culture prospers.
There are Chinni Peru, Yuan China;
Forbidden City is founded in Beijing.
True Pure Land Sect appears in Japan,
and the Chinese Opera emerges.

The Aztecs arise,
the Incas come forth,
Mexico City is founded.
Christians are in Ethiopia.
Tiantan Shrine is started,
and Ming is in China.

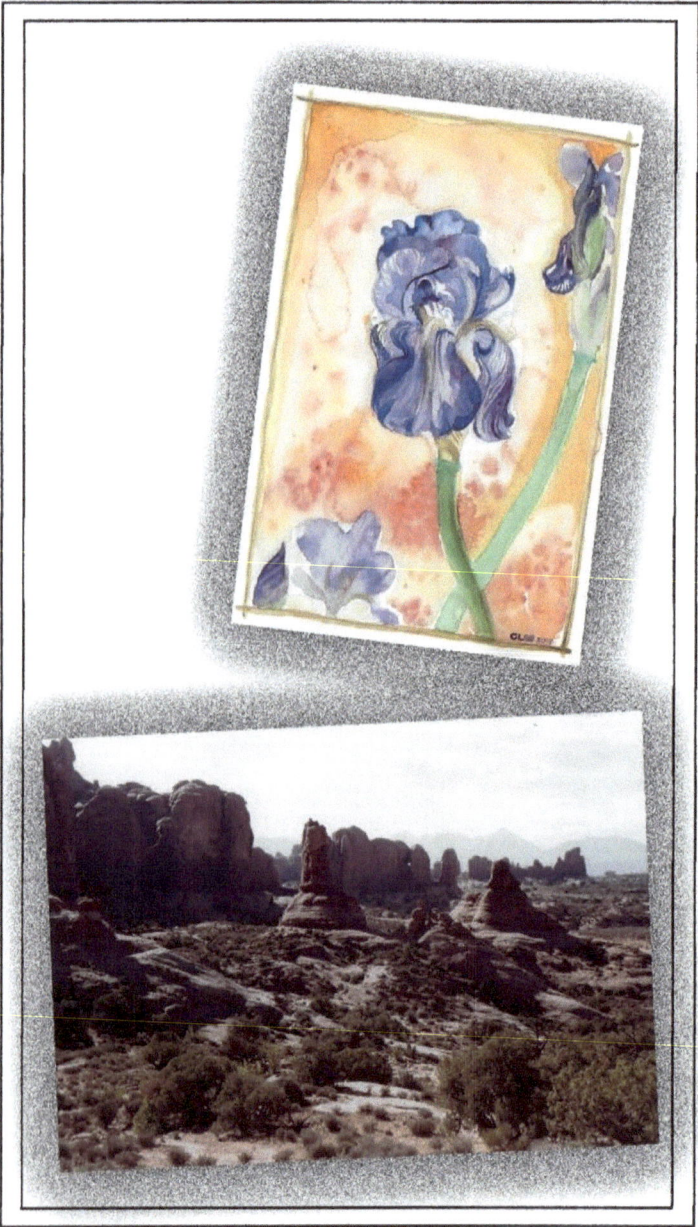

1400 to 1600

Tzarist Russia develops.
Constantinople has fallen.
There is renaissance in Europe.
Zheng He sails the Eastern oceans.
The Jains build a temple at Ranpur.
Movable type is invented by Koreans
whose armada founders against Japan,
where there is built the Kibitsu Shrine.
First witch hunting occurs inSwitzerland.
Brunelleschi returns perspective to canvas.
Gutenberg's press, and a rifle both appear.
The Madrass of Qaitbay is in Cairo, and
the Ueh Sherefeli Mosque, in Edirne.
A Comedia dell'arte emerges.
Bantu and Zulu civilizations
develop in south of Africa.
We know Medici, Borgia,
& the Malacca state.
There is Joan of Arc,
the War of the Roses,
Thomas Moore's Utopia,
the Tudor dynasty, and the
construction of Eaton College.
Malory tells of Mort d'Arthur.
We are graced by the lives of
Machiavelli, Donatello,
Shakespeare, Raleigh,
and Jan van Eyck.
Flemish paintings emerge.
The clavichord is invented,
and coffee is first brewed.

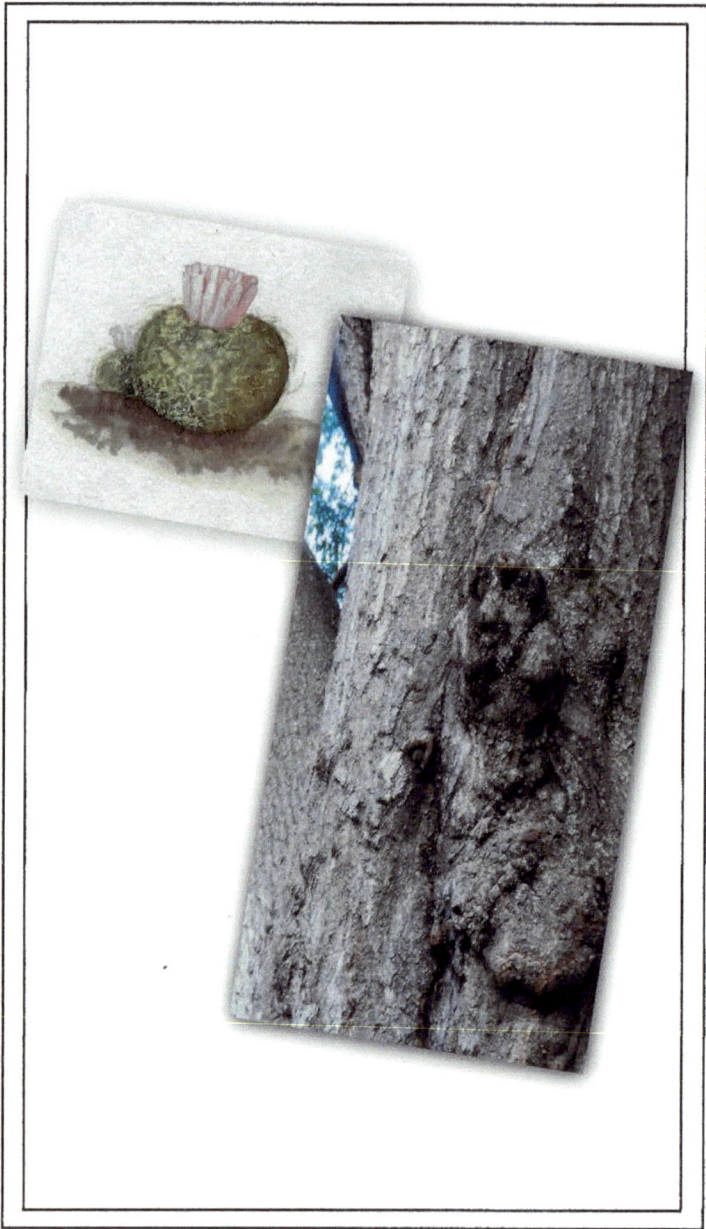

1400 to 1600 (2)

Spain is united, and
first flea circuses appear.
Mercator creates his map.
Also come four-masted carracks,
the quadrant for determining latitude,
Amerigo Vespucci, Christopher Columbus,
Vasco da Gama around the Cape of Good Hope &
Ponce de Leon seeks the fountain of youth.
Living root bridges are in Meghalaya, India.
Magellan circumnavigates the globe.
We know of Ignatius Loyola,
and Jesuits in South America.
We watch Spain and Portugal
'divide influence' over the earth,
Yongle collaborative Encyclopedia
& Jesters serving Montezuma
.

The Town Hall is built at Ghent.
Creators appear in the forms of
Cervantes, Leonardo da Vinci,
Raphael, El Greco,
Christine de Pisan.
A pendulum appears.
Comes Michelangelo
di Lodovico Buonarroti,
with the Sistine Chapel,
David, Moses, and La Pieta.
Raglan Castle towers above.
We know of Topkapi Palace.
St. Peter's becomes a cathedral.
Machu Picchu construction begins.

1400 to 1600 (3)

El Jadida Water Cisterns in Morocco.
Sanskore Mosque is built of mud, at
Timbuktu, on wooden scaffolding.
Tycho Brahe measures the planets.
We know Girolamo Savonarola,
Bramante, Erasmus, Francois
Rabelais, Pierre de Ronsard.
Beginning Reformation,
Martin Luther attends
a Diet of Worms.
Nobunaga Japan is
infiltrated by Portugal,
and Noh theatre matures.
The microscope is invented.
We see Andrea Palladio,
Monoyama architecture, and
the second recorded Supernova.

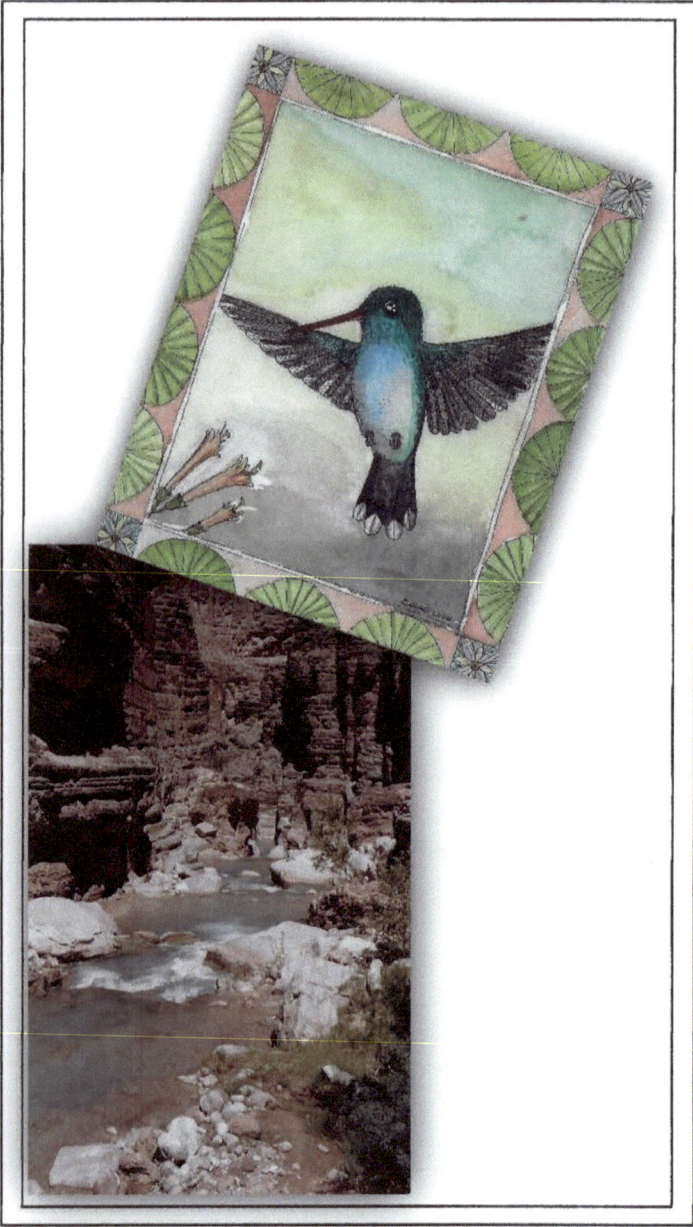

1400 to 1600 (4)

Andreas Vesalius is father of human anatomy.
Clowning becomes developed as a theatrical art form.
The Church of the Ascension towers over Moscow.
The Cathedral of the Virgin of the Intercession,
known now simply as St. Basil's, is built
in what is to become Red Square.
The Thulamela Venda, of South
Africa flourish in Empire.
We know Henry VIII,
Catherine of Aragon,
and the Huguenots.
The Moghul Akbar builds
Govind Deva Temple, Brindaban,
Wat Phra Sri Sarapet bell stupas.
Andean silver finances the world.
Tobacco is introduced to Europe.
Russia knows Ivan the Great, and
Macchu Picchu is built at 12,500 feet.
England defeats the Spanish Armada.
sabella d'Este is Marchese of Mantua.
The Ottoman Empire comes to zenith,
and Suleiman invades and expands.
Family Bernoulli founds a dynasty
with ten giants of mathematics.
Spain out laws Indian slavery,
only to introduce
slavery of Africans
to the West Indies.
Six million indigenous
new world inhabitants
die of European diseases
during the next fifty years.

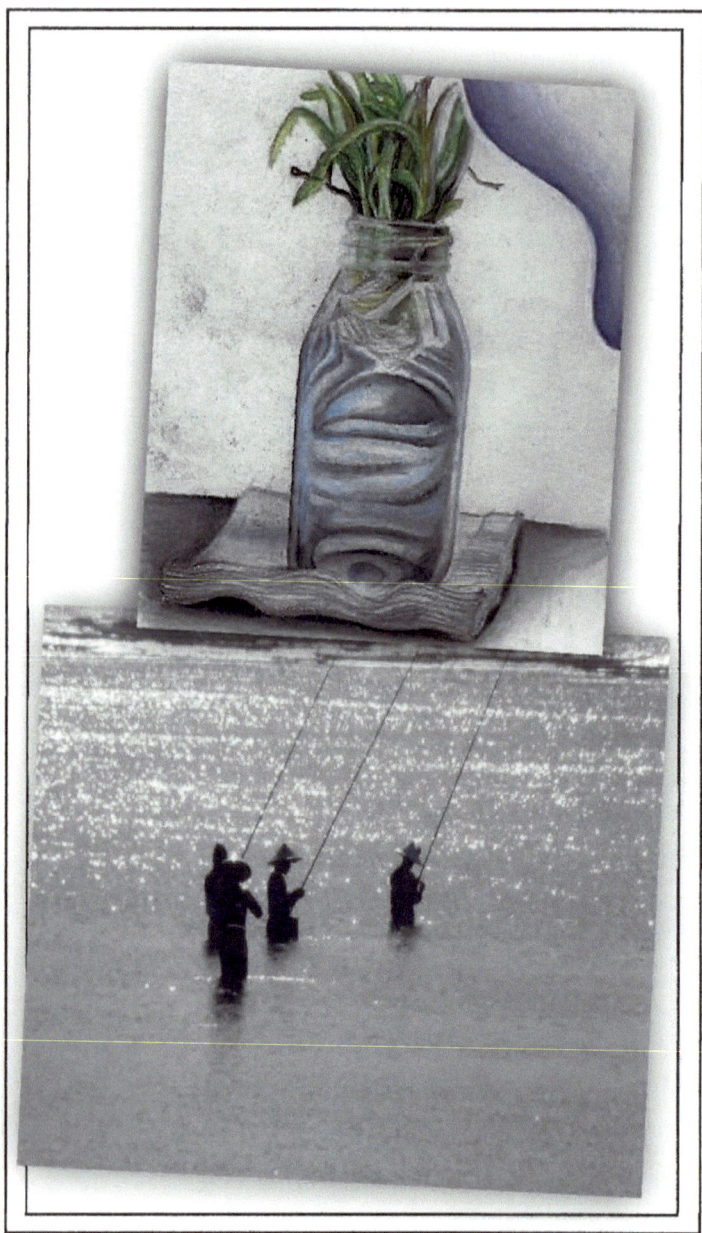

1400 to 1600 (5)

Decimals appear in math, while
(x) and (y) are introduced algebra.
A musical interval the third, appears.
The suspension coach is invented,
and coal is used for primary fuel.
The violin gains her maturity.
We witness the discoveries of,
zinc mercury, bismuth, cobalt,
nickel, & mass production.
Sikhism is founded.
Akbar conquers Orissa.
The Urdu Language matures.
A Tomb of Humayun is at Deli.
Mogul, and Sufvid India develop.
We see Songhai empires in Africa;
experience the maturing Shi'ite sect.
The Aztecs make a marvelous calendar.
There are also Copernicus, Galileo Galilei.
Kepler describes the motion of the planets.
Spain absorbs Portugal as Inquisition grows.
The Inca complete the Saqsaywaman fortress.
There are Montezuma, Cortez, and Pizarro.
Westminster Abbey glorifies fan vaulting.
Brazil, and Venezuela become colonized.
René Descartes declares all is thought.
Francisco Sanchez, opposes Aristotle
claiming that "Nothing is known".
Potatoes are imported to Europe.
The 'water closet' is invented.
Balboa discovers the Pacific,
as De Soto discovers more.
In England are Elizabeth I,
Drake, and Francis Bacon.

1600 to 1800

Elizabeth Regina leaves us and
there are Thirty Years of war.
Manchu Quin takes China
next to the 20th century.
The Palais de Versailles is
bequeathed by Louis XIV.
People learn about things:
Davy and the electric lamp,
Cartesian analytic geometry,
microscopic life by Leeuwenhoek,
Reflecting Telescope by Lippershy,
circulation of our blood by Harvey.
We give names to 'Galilean' satellites.
A 'curiosity' of scientists includes:
Pierre de Fermat, Pascal, Cavalieri,
Gregory, Rolle, Hudde, Huygens.
Potala Palace is rebuilt at Lhasa.

Our footprints are made
in time with the Mosque of
the Sultan Ahmed in Istanbul;
Mausoleum of Taj Mahal at Agra.
We know Maria Gaetana Agnesi:
a fine 'Beehive' village near Aleppo,
the great tomb of Akbar at Sikandra.
The first woman professor is at a university.
America's Georgia is founded by Oglethorpe.
Brook Taylor, as de Moivre, explores gambling

1600 to 1800 (2)

We are: Scarlatti, Pirendel, Duarte, Bononcini.
European chess has both rook and castle.
A Swahili mosque is at Gedi, Kenya.
Baroque defines music,
and our architecture,
with a 'chorus' of composers:
Rameau, Lully, de Cabazon,
Albioni, Zelenka, Germiniani,
Stolzel, Telemann, and Purcell.
Yiddish theatre appears.
Qing is in China and
Matteo Ricci brings
her philosophy.
We experience
a museum an,
opera house,
Rembrandt.
In Russia is Godunov.
The world population
is a half a billion.

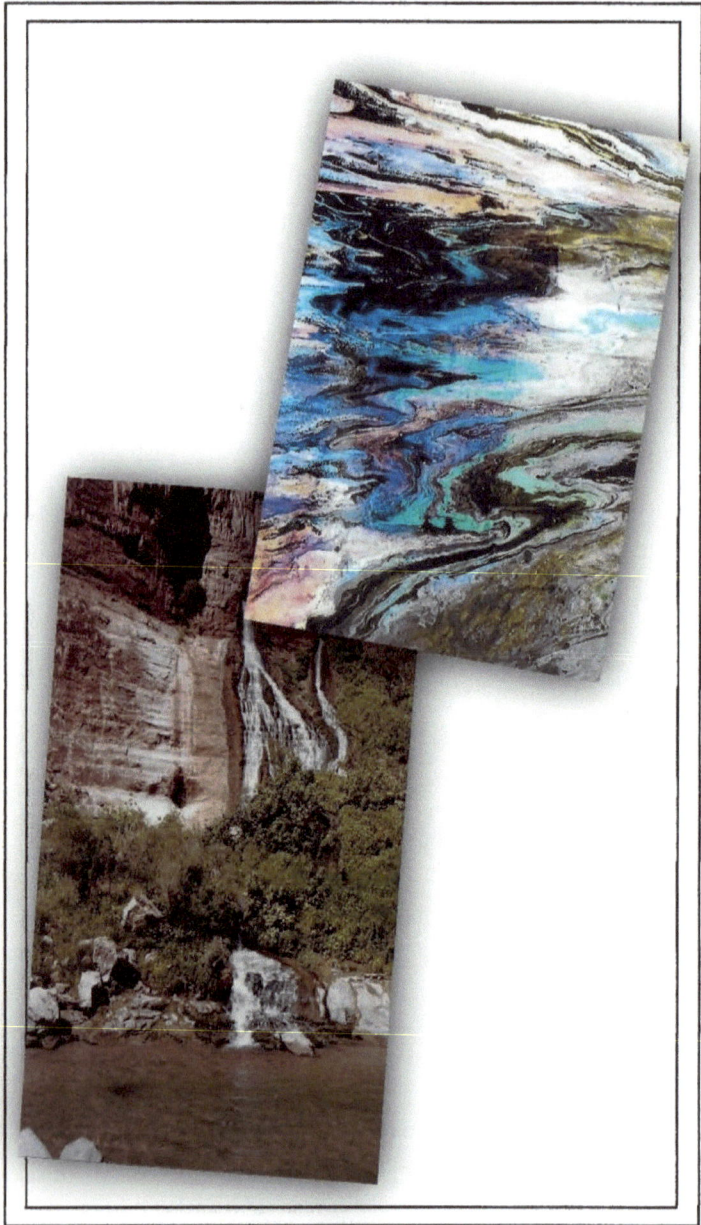

1600 to 1800 (3)

In Strasbourg, Germany,
humans use a mercantile
coinage system with banks,
in Amsterdam, and London,
forming joint stock companies
with issues of letters of credit.
See a first circus and clown act.
American theatre forms in
Williamsburg, VA, as is a
playhouse in New York.
Companies grow called:
East and West India,
Dutch West Africa.
A first Mayflower
sails with Pilgrims
to North America.
Our people create
the pendulum clock.
Sacagawea guides us.
Cromwell has England.
Our industry exploits coal,
air pumps, calculating machines,
the barometer, and the slide rule.
The printed newspaper, *Relation*,
is presented by Johann Carolus.
'Plot' will name a first dinosaur bone.
Slave dancing pounds in Congo Square, *NOLA*.
Experiment and repeatability lead the journals.
We see the church of the Intercession at Fili.
We are enchanted by Monteverdi, Corelli,
Laplace, Flamsteed, and Hooke. Halley,
and Newton struggle over our tides.
We have made the fugue, and ballet.
Anna Maria van Schurman paints.
English and French languages
spread with exploration,
and Louis XIV.

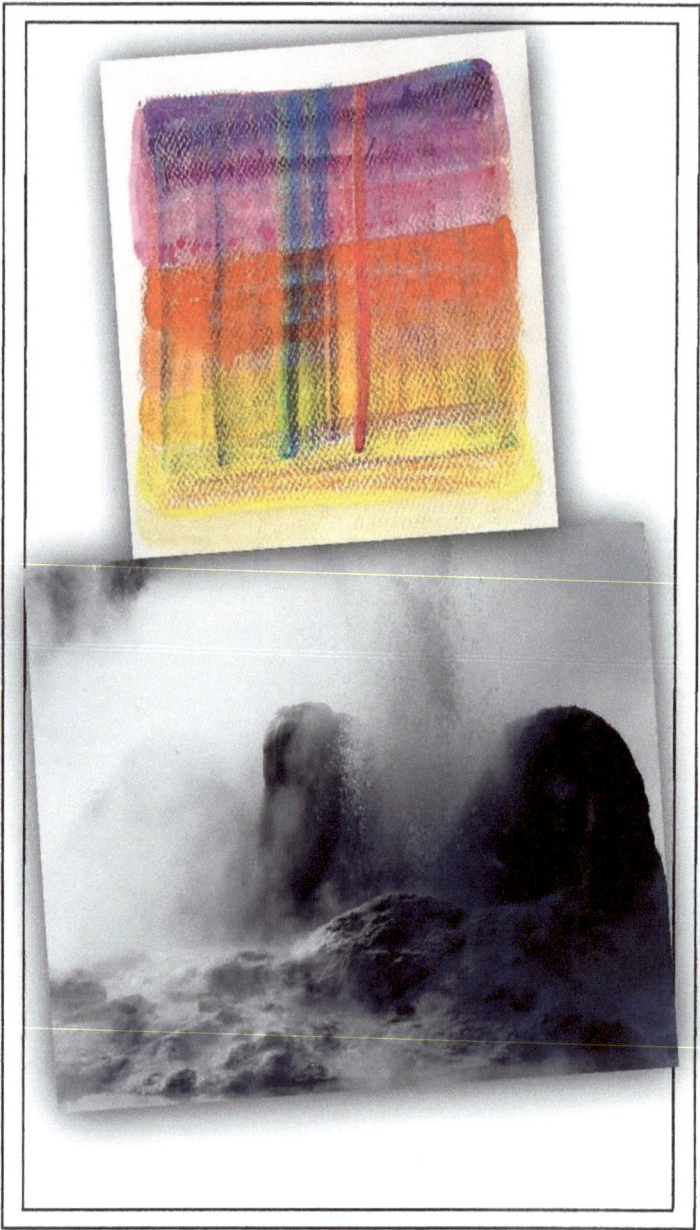

1600 to 1800 (4)

We know of Pascal, and Romanov Russia.
Jamestown and Manhattan are founded,
and in the north, Canada is colonized.
In Africa is the Oyo Kingdom.
In South Africa is 'apartheid',
found long before its name.
L'harmonie universelle
is given by Mersenne.
Spain rules California.
The Dodo is extinct.
Santa Fe is founded.
Europe finds Australia.
In Manchu, China is
Cao Xueqin's, *The Story of Stone.*
Artemisia Gentileschi paints for us.
Notice Leibniz vs Newton vs Calculus.
A sextant creates maps from the stars.
The Summer Palace is built in Beijing.
Soil is turned by a moldboard plow.
During the Tokugawa Shogunate,
comes to us Basho's haiku, and
Japan begins isolating herself.
There is also color printing.
Giordano Bruno is burned
at the Inquisition stake
for declaring that the
universe is infinite.
We gather together
a Society of Friends,
and discover Uranus
and republics emerge in
Batavia, Helvitica, Cisaipine,
Liguria, America, and France.
Elements are organized by Boyle.

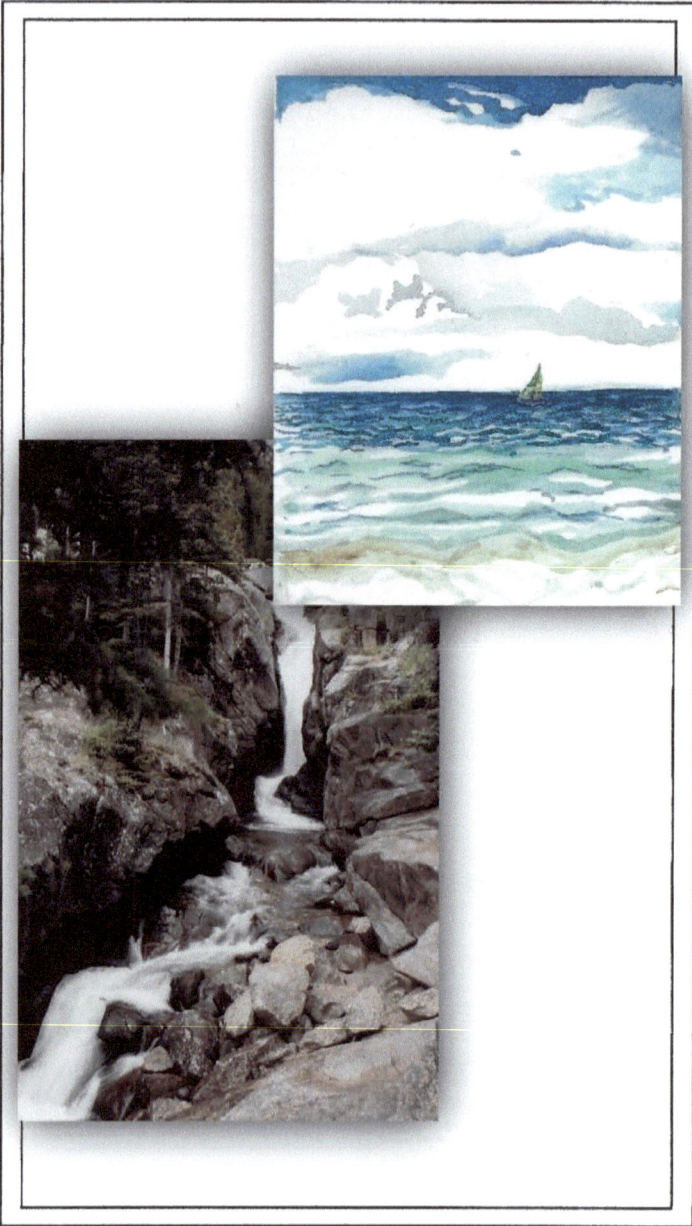

1600 to 1800 (5)

We are introduced to
Edmond Halley, Stradivari,
Swift, Franklin, and Lavoisier.
The speed of light is calculated.
The press presents its own power.
The Rococo riot develops, and in
London there is plague and fire.
In England the common lands
are becoming enclosed, and
Wren begins his work on
St. Paul's Cathedral.
'electric" is coined;
William Gilbert
Spain Restores;
a war of Succession.
Colonies are founded at
Hudson, and Massachusetts.
There are witch trials in Salem.
We know Bernini and Boromini.
We experience the arrival of
Greenwich Observatory,
and hot air balloons.
Jethro Tull invents the seed drill.
The first lodge of Freemasons is founded,
the New York Stock Exchange is established,
the harpsichord emerges, the pianoforte is invented,
the trio sonata is developed, music grows so the
orchestra emerges, and the concerto appears.
China expands her borders and influence.
Moscow University is established.
Brasilia becomes the Capitol.
The Easter Island megaliths
are discovered, as are
the Bering Straits.

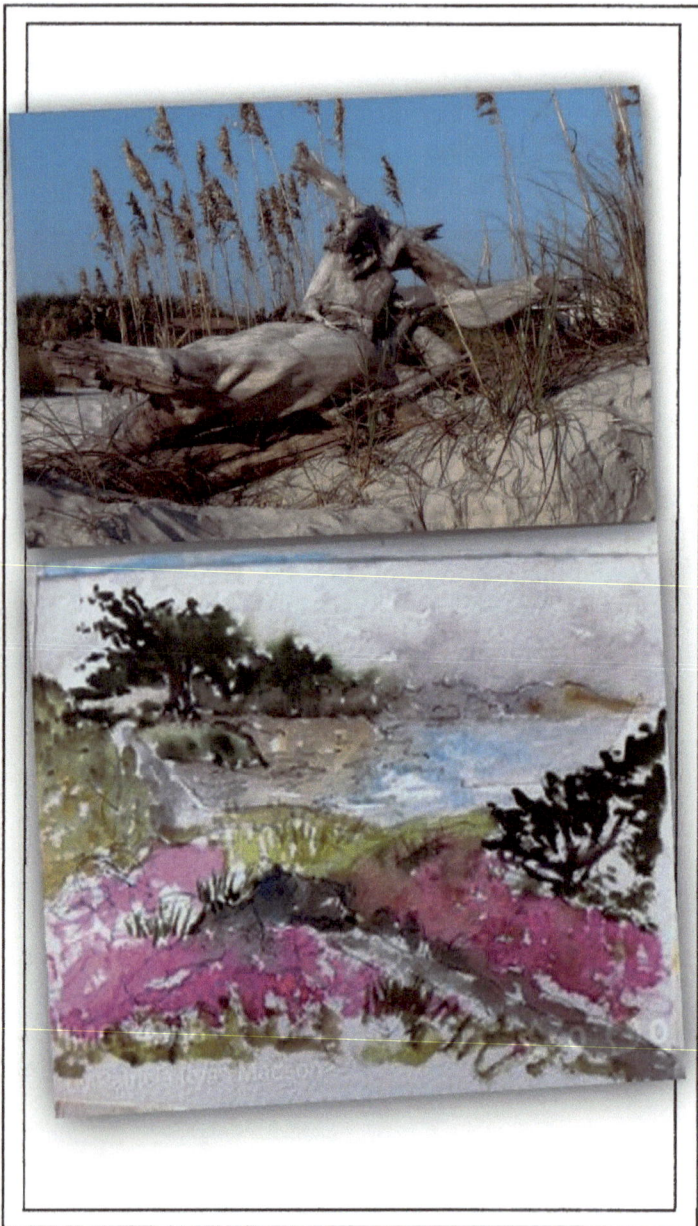

1600 to 1800 (6)

Comes an Enlightenment,
gravity, mathematics, and physics,
and a universe in the image of a machine.
Rousseau comes forth with a Social Contract.
We are Voltaire, William Penn, Margaret Brent,
Wesley, Racine, Anne Bradstreet, Moliere,
Montesquieu, Locke, Hume, Spinoza,
Berkeley, Kant, Hobbs, Malthus,
Defoe, Paine, Adam Smith, and
the pirate Anne Bonny.

St. Petersburg is founded.
Peter the Great is in Russia,
Frederick II is in Prussia, and
then there is Catherine the Great.
There are the Ashanti in West Africa,
and the Cross River Monoliths, while
Bantu East Africa begins to flourish.
Burma blossoms; Rio de Janeiro too.
In France are Napoleon Bonaparte,
MacLaurin, Sophie Buckland,
and Hans Christian Ørsted.
The Rosetta Stone is found.
The world Population is
900 Million.

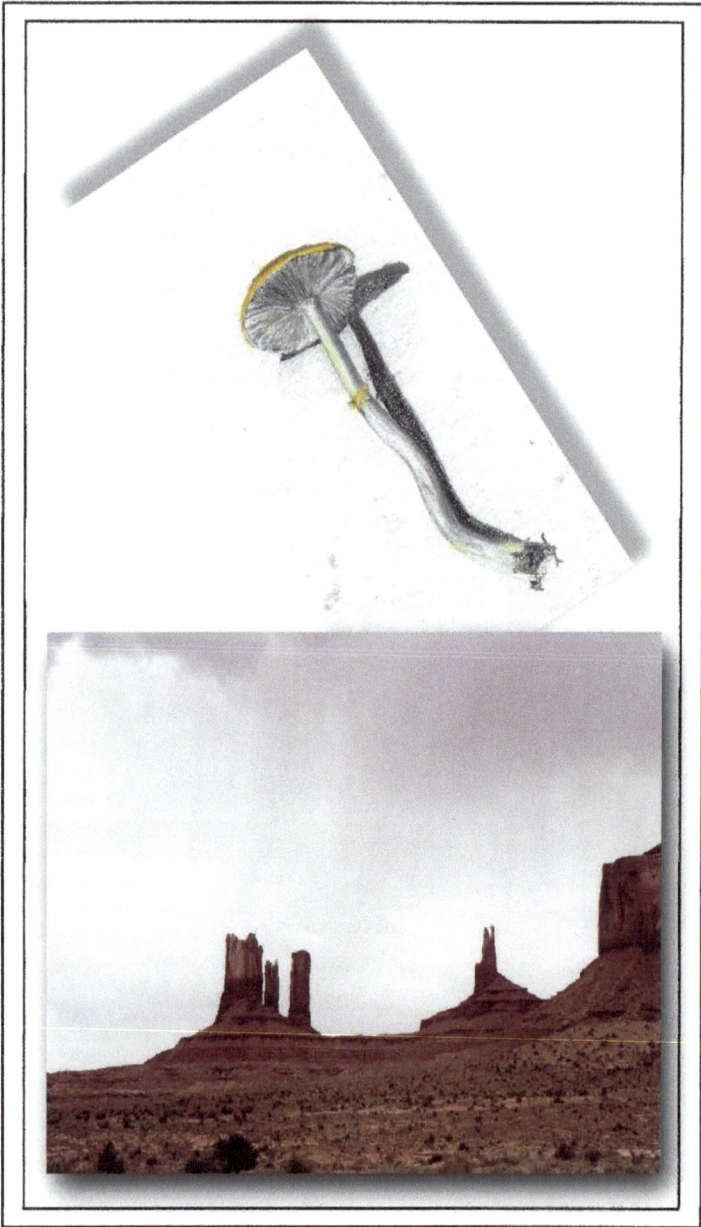

1600 to 1800

Linnaeus classifies botanicae.
Begins the industrial revolution.
The steam engine, the cotton gin,
flying shuttle and spinning jenny
are among the many inventions.
Discoveries include
rubber, carbon dioxide,
hydrogen, oxygen, nitrogen,
tungsten, isolated hydrogen gas,
coal gas light, and current electricity.
Other new things include the threshing
machine, the battery, and the sextant.
We know the first public utilities,
Harrison's chronometer gives
the longitude fixed at sea.
A Balloon flight crosses
the English Channel.
Jenner inoculates
smallpox for us.
Ba'al Shem Tov
gives us Hassid.

Neoclassicism is
enlivened by lives of
Mendelssohn, Goethe,
Bach, Hayden, Handel,
Mozart, Beethoven, Vivaldi,
Shelly, Mary Wollstonecraft,
Wordsworth, Coleridge, Keates,
Abigail Adams, and Jane Addams,
John Herschel, Whewell Lagrange,
Benjamin Banneker, Leonard Euler.
Jeanne Labrosse fill the air in balloons.
Saint Simon's Utopian Socialists appear.
Jupiter Hammon is published in America,
and there is the Jefferson Constitution.

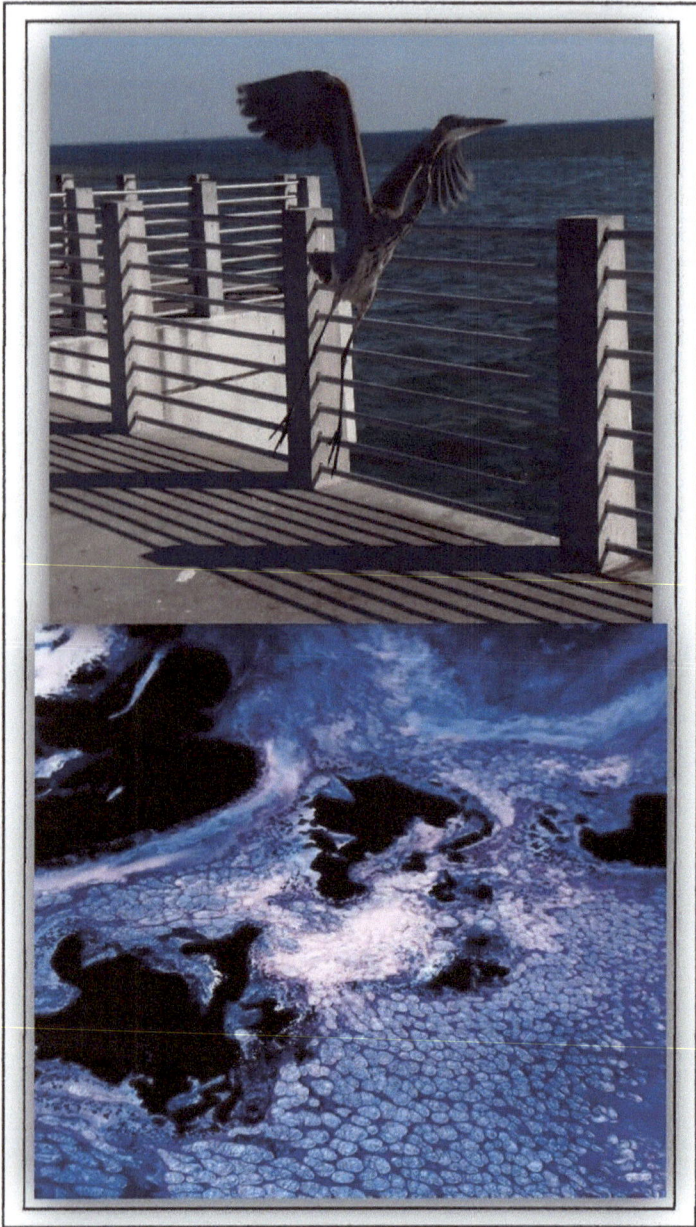

1800 to 1900

Augusta Ada, Countess of Lovelace, forms an algorithm.
A new century comes with Code Napoleon,
Bank of France, the Congress of Vienna;
a little corporal is at Waterloo, and Elba.
Mathematicians gather and expand with
Laplace, Cauchy, Gauss, Bernhard Riemann,
Neils Henrik, Sir William Hamilton, Jacobi,
Peirce, George Boole, Charles Dodgson,
with double duty as Lewis Carroll.
Plasma is discovered.
The Iguanodon is identified.
Robert Elsworth Lowe is born.
J.J. Thompson discovers the electron.
Émilie Du Châtelet translates *Principia.*
Megalosaurus named by William Buckland.
Scott Joplin, Buddy Bolden, Tom Turpin play.
Eliza Burton 'Lyda' Conley is the first Indigenous
American woman to plea before SCOTUS.
We complete the change from
a feudal to a Euro-colonial planet.
England takes a Cape of Good Hope,
rebuilds a Palace of Westminster, and
prospers under opium trade in China.
Independence is achieved at once in
Belgium, Poland, Haiti, Paraguay,
Brazil, Venezuela, Peru,
Mexico, and Uruguay.
The Netherlands and
Singapore are founded.
Romanticism comes with
Audubon, Leopardi, Goya, Delacroix,
Fairy Tales by the brothers Grimm,
Victor Hugo, Schumann,
Richard Strauss, Bartok,
Rossini, von Weber,
Chopin, and
Byron.

1800 to 1900

Discoveries include
fossils of the dinosaurs,
electricity physics by Volta,
electrical induction by Farady,
the unit of electricity by Ampere,
Ohm's law, potassium, sodium, and
a metal plate photography by Niepce.
We learn from Elizabeth Blackwell, Ethel
Smyth, Margaret Sanger, Elizabeth Magie,
Nettie Stevens, and Margaret Knight.
Dalton founds organic chemistry;
theory of atoms is established.
The Cathedral at Cologne is
completed after 600 years.

Inventions produce:
steamboat, locomotive,
and the first steam railroad:
solenoids, and thermocouples,
gas light, canned food, artificial ice,
auto punch card fabric production,
screw cutting machines, and lathes,
vulcanized rubber via Goodyear,
and a Samuel Morse telegraph.
Ultraviolet light is discovered.
The lawn mower is invented.
There are electromagnets and
electromagnetism by Maxwell.
Louisiana Territory is purchased;
Lewis & Clark explore a vastness.
Non-Euclidian geometry develops.
The canal is completed from Erie as,
the Monroe Doctrine is established.
There are the noetics of Ramanujan,
as well as Lobachevsky, Srinivasa
and Sofia Kovalevskaya.

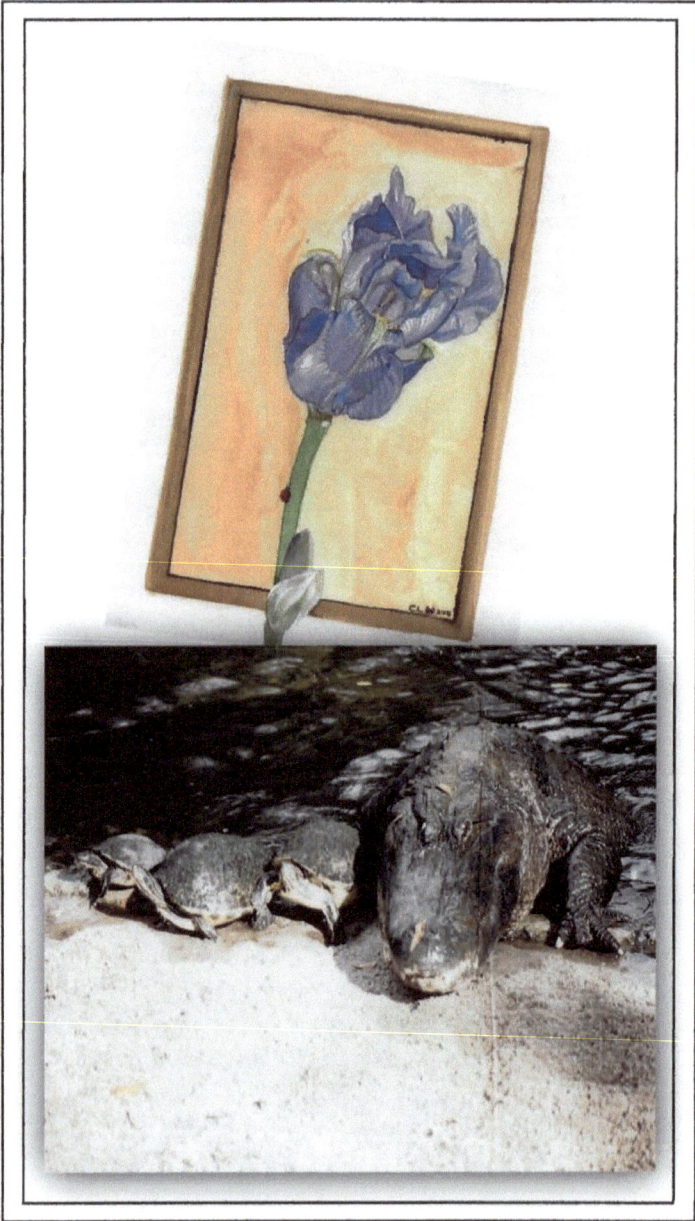

1800 to 1900 ₍₃₎

The British Empire
ends its slavery in 1833.
The Colt pistol is invented.
Human creativity expands as:
George Sand, Dickinson, Glinka,
Stendhal, Comte, Balzac, Pushkin,
John Smith with the angel Moroni.
We see Hokusai's Mount Fuji prints;
also a deciphering of Cuneiform script.
Tecumseh, Red Cloud, Sitting Bull, and
Crazy Horse resist European invasion.
Clifton Suspension Bridge is in Bristol.
Scarpa is building. Aspirin is invented.
HRH Queen Victoria begins her reign
over the English that will name an era.
Revolutions of 1848 engage humans in
Spain, Portugal, Paris, Venice, Vienna,
Berlin, Milan, Warsaw, and Prague.
August Mobius provides a surface;
two-dimensional, non-orientable.
Elizabeth Cady Stanton presents
the Declaration of Sentiments at
Women's Rights Convention.
Bolivar is in South America.
In England we are charmed by
the Brontes, and the Brownings.
Louisa May Alcott is in America
In Texas, the siege of the Alamo.
Mehemet Ali Pasha rules Egypt.
The African interior is explored.
Liberia is founded as a colony
of liberated American slaves.
China knows opium wars.
Mary Ellen Pleasant, and
Eliza Anna Grier
advance us all.

1800 to 1900 (4)

Explorations of the mind brings us
Darwin, John Stewart Mill, Hegel,
Dickens, Tennyson, Hawthorn,
Thoreau, Whitman, Melville,
Kierkegaard,
de Tocqueville,
Wagner, and Verdi.
We begin a Suez Canal.
The steamship Savannah
crosses the Atlantic, and
in the Crimea there is war.
America acquires California,
Texas, and New Mexico.
We lionize the settling
of the American West.
Elizabeth Blackwell is
first woman physician.
Modern Paganism appears.
Lister revolutionizes surgery.
First sound recorded by Scott.
A Rotary printing press is invented.
Pasteur demonstrates antibiotic effect.
Explorations of the mind are represented by
Bahaullah, Brook Farm, Schopenhauer, Flaubert,
Tolstoy, Baudelaire, Whistler, Gounod, Garibaldi,
Marx, Engels, and The Communist Manifesto.
Anesthesia is advanced by Crawford Long.
Urbanization brings the London subway,
The Yoshimitsu Shogunate opens Japan.
In Paris there are sewers.
A cable is transatlantic.
Oil is discovered.

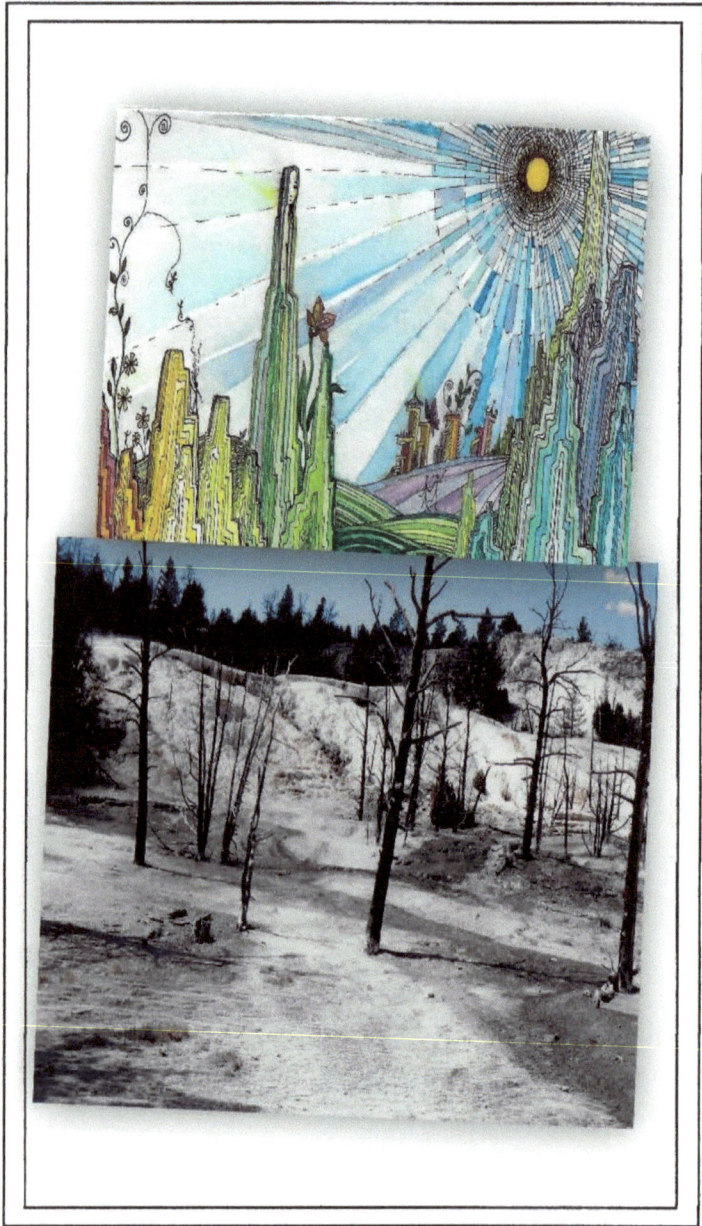

1800 to 1900 ₍₅₎

Freedom is championed by
Nat Turner, Harriet Beecher Stowe,
Sojourner Truth, Harriet Tubman,
John Brown, and Dred Scott.
Japan engages in a civil war.
The Americans do likewise.
Slavery ends in US in 1865.
Lincoln is assassinated.
Industrialization brings
Bessemer Steel, the Gatling gun;
as well as iron ships. MIT is founded.
The dominion of Canada is established.
European invaders force the resettlement
of North American indigenous peoples.
Humans participate in a trail of tears.
Inventions by the people include
daguerreotype photography,
first plastic- celluloid,
the sewing machine,
washing machine,
breech loading,
and long-distance rifles.
Some discoveries include
Neptune, and nitroglycerin.
The Great Exhibit at the Crystal Palace
remains triumphant of human progress.
St. Pancras Station in London supports
railroads across the UK, and
trade unions are developing.
Turgenev composes for us.
Republics are established
in France, Rome, Venice and Hungary.
Social Security is in Bismarck's Germany.
We see the New German Empire,
the first postage stamps,
Australia colonized,
and a British Raj.

1800 to 1900 (6)

Europeans dominate Asia, and
African colonization continues.
France colonizes Indochina, and
the Antarctic coast is discovered.
See the Meiji Japanese reformation.
Jujitsu is founded, Judo develops, and
The New York Philharmonic is formed.
Bouchet has first PhD in physics.
Julia Smith translates a Bible.
The search for beauty brings:
Beaux arts, the opera in
Paris and Vienna, and
the Statue of Liberty.
Faraday illuminates
a path of electricity.
Inventions come:
the cathode ray tube, gyroscope,
spectroscope, microphone, steel furnace,
modern elevator, the Maxim machine gun,
steel alloy, typewriter, barbed wire,
steam turbines, and dynamite
brought to us by Alfred Nobel.
Exploration in science is extended
by Mendel, Mendeleev, and Doppler.
America manifests her destiny, and
a transcontinental railway is completed.
In Africa is colonization of the interior.
Clara Barton founds The Red Cross.
Standard Oil is founded, and
world-wide cartels expand.

There is a Sino-Japanese war.
Korea gains her Independence.
Asia begins to assimilate the West.
200,000 Chinese emigrate to America.
Our experience is: Florence Nightingale,
Liszt, Johann Strauss, Offenbach, Brahms,
Frederick Douglas, Booker T. Washington.
We are reading: Kipling, Rodin, Dostoevsky,
Ibsen, Shaw, Wilde, Hardy, and Nietzsche.
Comes Blavatsky's Theosophical Society,
Mary Baker Eddy; Christian Science, and
sound's origins of Jazz, and Blues music.
Australians experiences a Wild West.
Impressionism is offered to our eyes,
and hearts by Monet, Manet,
Van Gough, Renoir, Degas,
Klimt, and Rossetti.
Japanese wood block prints mature,
the Fabian Society is founded, and
in Oklahoma there is a land rush.
Women vote in Australia in 1861,
and in New Zeland in 1893.
Slavery ends in Brazil in 1888.
Social Darwinism and racism erupt in the West.
The first US union - Knights of Labor - is established.
We hear the call for Workers of the World to Unite.
We see anti-Semitism, and The Basle Convention.
P.T. Barnum brings The Greatest Show on Earth.
There are Robber Barons;
Gould, Rockefeller, and
Morgan among them.
Bacteria is identified.
Technology bears names of new things:
automobile by Daimler and Benz,
a phonograph, piezoelectricity,
radio by Hertz, motion pictures,
the refrigerator, aluminum,
and the pneumatic tire

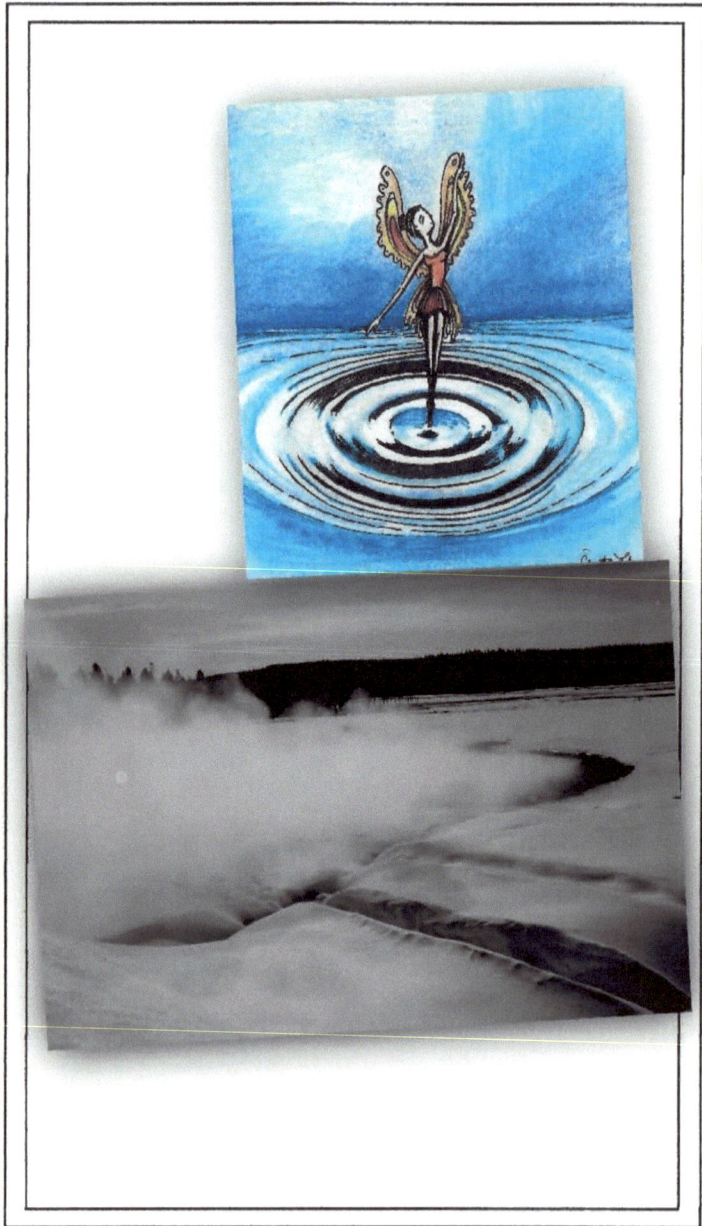

1800 to 1900 (8)

Art Nouveau is introduced by
Moreau, Van Gogh, Pissarro,
Gaugin, Munch, Cezanne,
Beardsley, and Gaudi,
who began work on
The Church of the
Sagrada Familia.
Benin African art develops,
and we become familiar with
Rimsky-Korsakov, Debussy,
Mahler, Tchaikovsky, Sibelius,
Sirs Gilbert and Sullivan,
John Philip Sousa, and,
Scott Joplin giving us his
gift of ragtime jazz in music.
Our minds are expanded with
Freud, Mark Twain, Zola, Yeats,
Chekov, de Maupassant, Nabokov,
Kropotkin, Stanislavski, Strindberg.
There is a terrible
flood in Johnstown.
In our hearts, chaos.
In journalism we know
Hurst, Pulitzer, Scripps, Ochs,
Yellow Journalism, and Nelly Bly.
Herzl founds the Zionist movement.
An Alliance called Triple is formed by
Germany, Austria-Hungary, and Italy.
Hans Christian Anderson tells us farey tales.
Krakatoa erupts and covers the earth with ash.
In science, find Max Weber, Thomas E. Edison,
Marie and Pierre Curie, Michelson and Morley

1800 to 1900 (9)

Some inventions and discoveries are
diphtheria antitoxin, Coca Cola,
Bell's telephone, Eastman film,
the Lumiere projector, and
an electricity run trolley.
Some discoveries include
a diesel-powered engine,
radioactivity, electrons,
and x-rays by Röentgen.

America Federates Labor.
Reliance Building reaches
for the sky in Chicago, and
Sherman enacts Antitrust.
Boxers are in Rebellion and
A Bridge grows in Brooklyn.
Eifel's tower lifted to the sky.
Peace is conferred at The Hague.
Hong Kong is leased to the British.
Balfour leads a Parliament for 20 years.
The English and the Boers develop war, and
Spanish and Americans make war in the west.
Samuel Clemens, and Geronimo walk the earth.
The Russians are at war with Japan, and
Alexander II of Russia is assassinated.
The modern Olympics are founded.
The Population of world is
1.6 Billion.

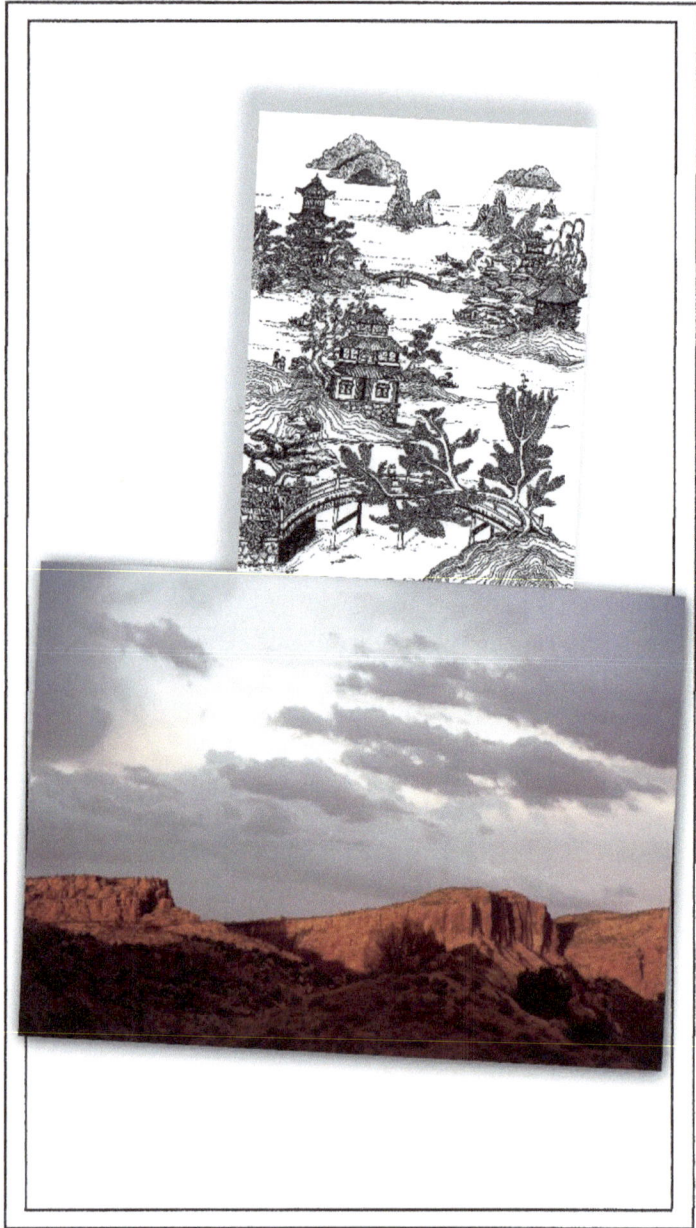

1900 to 1950

Victoria is gone.
Long live the King.
Aswan Dam is opened.
We experience the lives of
Kier Hardie,
Rachmaninoff,
Teilhard de Chardin,
Moussorgsky, Chaliapin,
Marconi, Tesla, Max Planck,
Diaghiliv, Stravinsky, Fokine,
Hofmann, and von Hoffmansthal.
Juliette Low founds the Girl Scouts.
Winifred Ward founds Creative Drama.
Power given to the people, first in England.
Arthur Nobel's Prize tries to amend dynamite.
People begin to study an endocrine system, and
the British launch a dreadnought battleship.
New York has Grand Central Terminal,
and The Woolworth Building is
the tallest structure in the world.
Pankhurst founds
The National Women's Social Political Union.
Smith College plays first women's Basketball Team.
We know Alice Guy-Blaché, and Maud Wagner.
The Commonwealth of Australia is created.
The North and South Poles are reached.
We have Russian anti-Jewish pogroms.
The Minoan Culture is rediscovered.
Improvisational theatre reemerges
with Moreno in New York.
We leave earth as the
Wright Brothers fly.
Jensen-Klint builds
Grundtvig in Copenhaven

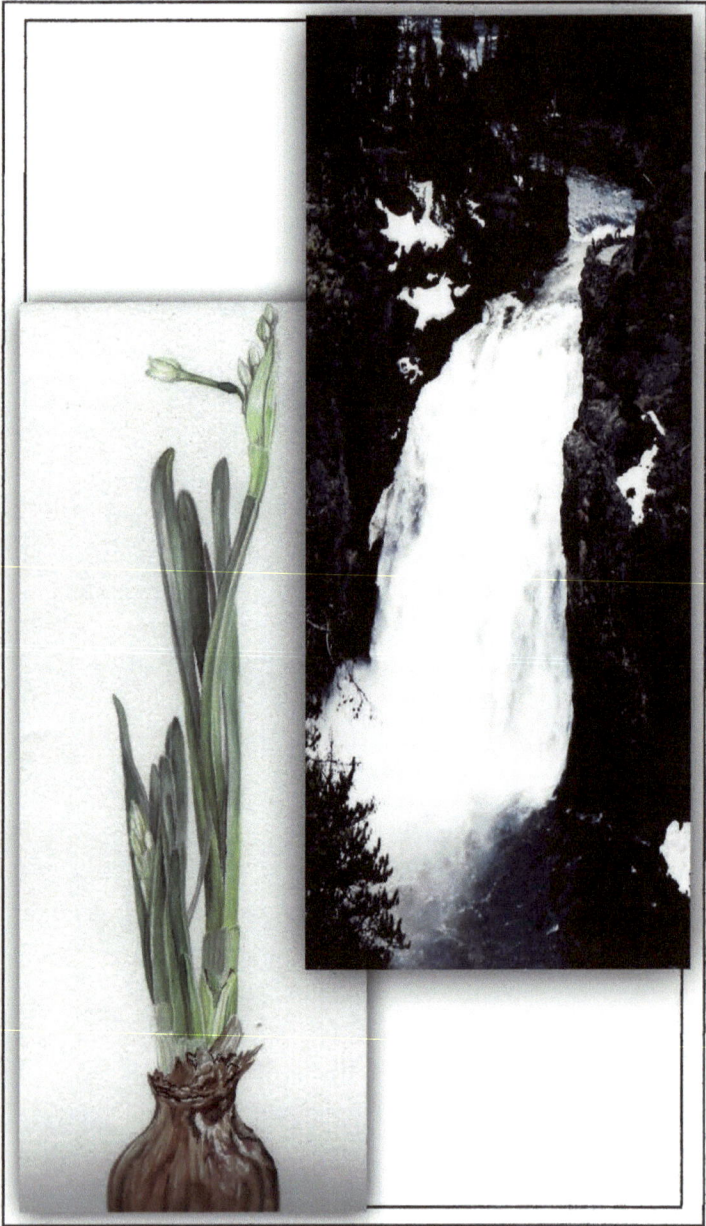

1900 to 1950

Bakelite is developed.
Japan and Russia make war, and
Rolls Royce Corporation is founded.
Broadway Tunnel opens Manhattan.
In France is a 10-hour work day, and
the separation of church and state.
Lindstrom Company is created,
manufacturing and marketing
phonographs and Phono-records.
Mount Wilson Observatory is made.
A 3,000 carat 'Cullinan' diamond is found.
In Europe are: Ravel, Pavlova, and Karsavina.
Nijinsky dances Le Sacre du Prentemps.
Earth quakes in San Francisco, Messina,
Avezzano, Martinique, Tokyo, and Gansu.
Mathematics is being applied to everything
and produces an early 20th Century bouquet,
of Grace Chisholm Young, Gödel, Fisher,
Pearson, and Gardner.
Comes Susan B. Anthony.
Human suffrage triumphs in
Norway in 1913, Britain in 1918,
Germany in 1919, America in 1920,
and Brazil in 1930.
America empowers a
Pure Food and Drug Act.
HMS Dreadnought is launched
weighing 17,900 tons, at 21 knots.
The Pentecostal movement develops,
Women gain the vote in Australia.
The empire of the Ottoman
is handed out to all comers
with countries invented and
the seeds of new wars within.
Revolution is in China and Mexico.
We see the first transatlantic flight, and
mass spectrography expands range of vision.

1900 to 1950 (3)

Phenomenology is founded.
Ford produces en mass;
creates the Model A.
We fly 100 miles in
craft heavier than air.
Minkowski formulates
four-dimensional geometry.
Harrison cultures live tissue.
Radio sounds music & voice.
Morgan begins genetic research.
Perry and Henson Pole the north.
We talk peace at The Hague again.
Lumiere develops color photography.
Gertrude Ederle swims the Channel.
Browning has invented his revolver.
An auto across America in 65 days,
and we share combine harvesters.
Baseball has its first post season.
Comes the Chinese Republic.
Gamma rays are discovered.
The Teddy Bear is invented.
Cairo University founded.
Ammonia is synthesized.
We swirl first helicopters, and
build a future with the Citta Nuova.
In Chicago there is the Robie House.
We catch first recording of an opera.
We are *Women Airforce Service Pilots*;
Peltier's solo, Willa Brown flying.
F.W. Woolworth sets up shop.
Extensive emigration occurs;
Japanese, to Southeast Asia,
Europeans, to America

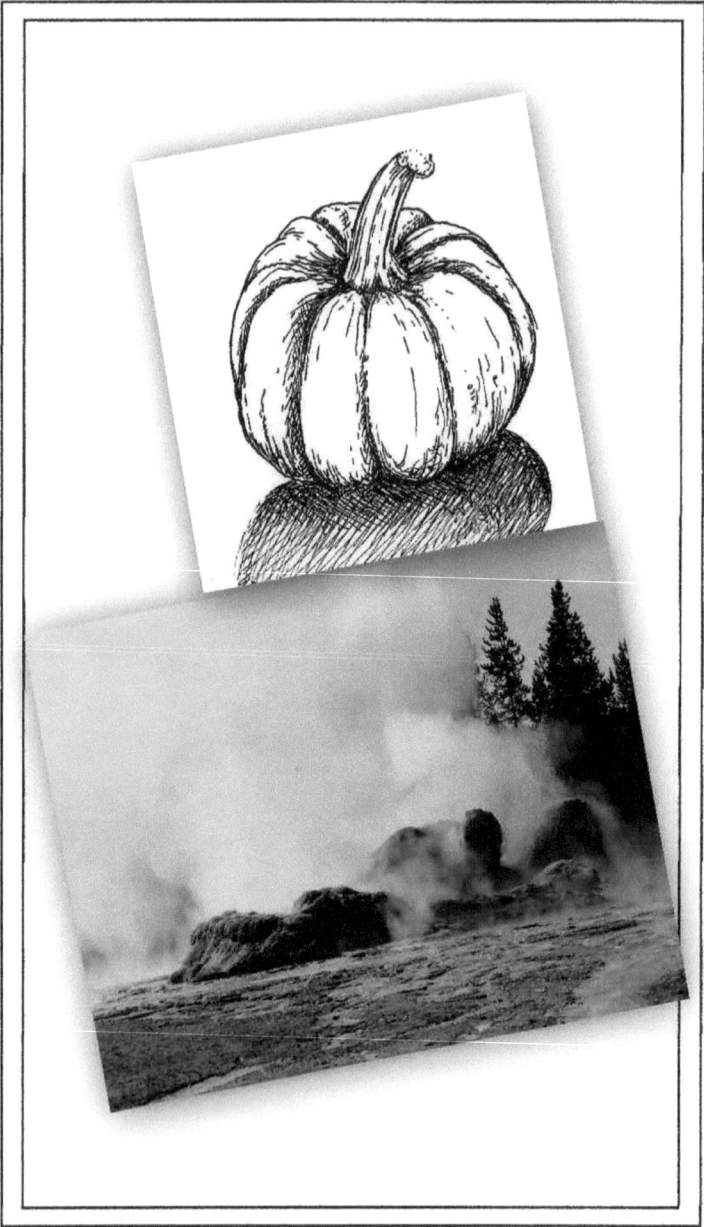

1900 to 1950 (4)

Silent movies arrive as
William Selig's first film,
The Count of Monte Christo.
The Panama Canal is completed,
costing just enough lives to fill a city.
an Anglo-Persian Oil Company is formed.
National Health is introduced into England.
Cubism comes with Gris, Klee, and Kandinsky.
A message is sent around the world in 12 minutes.
W.E.B. du Bois, et al give us the NAACP.
There are Mac Sennett, Harold Lloyd,
Charlie Chaplin, and Mary Pickford.
We are enriched by H. G. Wells,
Cecilia Payne-Gaposchkin,
Hughes, O'Casey, Yeats,
and Evangeline Booth.
Adrenaline is discovered.
Toson and Katai are in Japan.
Alliances form to make peace:
an Anglo-Japanese, Franco-Russian,
Entente Cordiale, Britain and France,
and with an Anglo-Russian Treaty.
The British Empire sets no more on:
India, Hong Kong, South Africa,
Australia, New Zealand, nor Canada.
Gorky sees a Russian reformation.
General Motors is incorporated.
Air flight reaches 12,800 feet.
Americans occupy 48 states.
Turing invents an Enigma.
Vitamins are identified.
Among inventions we find:
a gyrocompass, and cellophane,
a radiotelegraph across the Atlantic,
telegraphic transmission of photographs.

1900 to 1950 (5)

Zapata is in Mexico and
human reform comes with the rise of
Socialism, Communism, and Nationalism.
Probability, called a proton, is discovered.
A host of Nobel Prizes redefine much:
Stern, Curie with two sciences,
Pauli, Born, Dirac, vonLaue,
Plank, DeBroglie, Laporte,
Rutherford, Thompson,
and Ernest Lawrence.
Humans see Art Deco,
abstract, and Bauhaus:
Matisse, Ravel, Puccini,
Alfred North Whitehead,
Jung, Prokofiev, Melnikov,
Isadora Duncan, Sun Yat Sen,
Grace Abbott, Rankin, Adler,
Bertrand Russell, Archibald
MacLeash, and Von Neumann.
Morgan builds a castle for Hurst.
Ramon Y Cajal explores the brain.
Universal suffrage comes to Austria.
Bohr introduces quantum mechanics.
Albert Einstein proposes relativity.
Geiger invents a counter, and
Ford creates diesel tractors.
Stainless steel is developed.
Lawrence is in Arabia.
European monarchies are deposed,
or replaced, in a War of the World;
coming with battle at the Somme
and death en mass beyond grief.
Nikolai Lenin, and Trotsky, and
Russian Revolution precede
a League made of Nations.

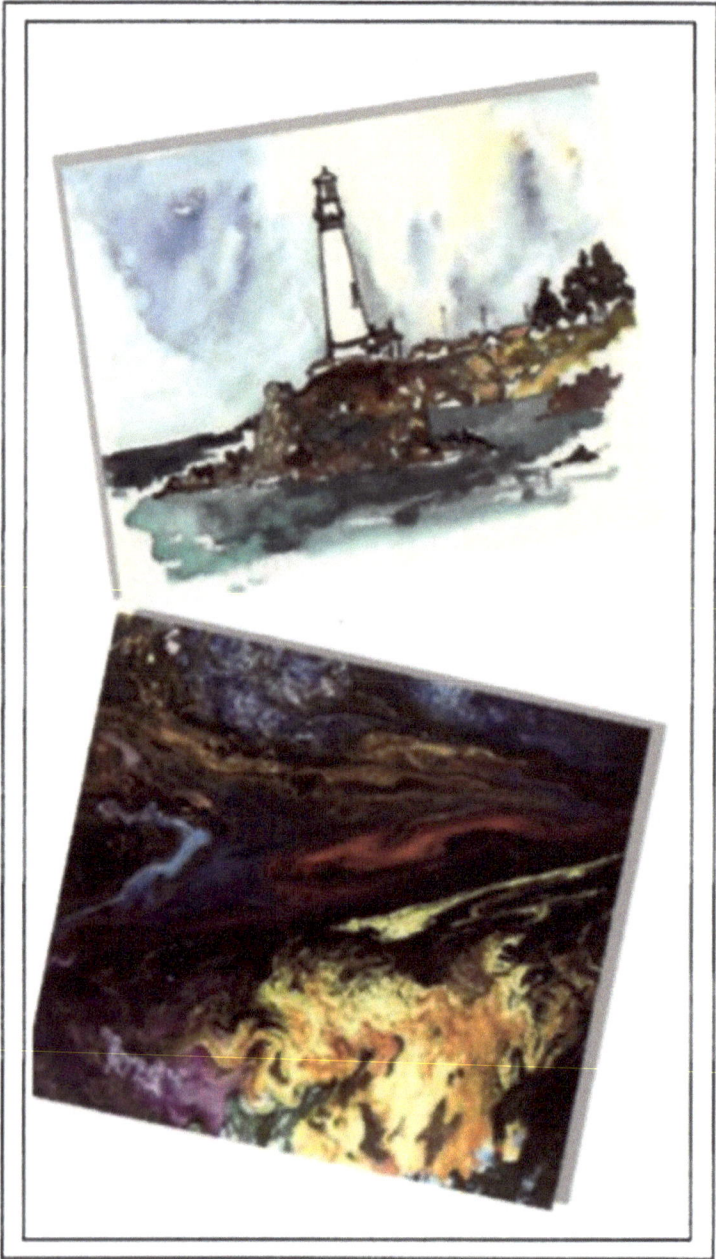

1900 to 1950 ₍₆₎

Hollywood sounds Al Jolson;
grows with deMille, Ford,
Brothers Warner, Capra,
and a family Barrymore.
Empire State Building is
the tallest structure ever.
America is in Prohibition
of alcohol, and regulating
drugs, and pharmaceuticals.
Hirohito is emperor of Japan.
Time is measured using atoms.
Radio networks are in America.
Josephine Baker sings and spies.
Existence of a top quark is confirmed.
Architecture becomes modern, bringing
Buckminster Fuller, Frank Lloyd Wright,
reflected by the Ecole des Beaux-Arts.
Genocide disgraces our languages and
Being; deaths of a million in Armenia.
World-wide, thirty million die from flu.
Chang Kai-Shek, and Mao Zedong appear.
Aimee Semple McPherson roams the airway.
Organized crime surfaces as a world power.
First British Labor Government appears.
There are labor actions throughout a
world engaging in industrialization.
Women begin coming to the fore:
Jeannette Rankin to Congress
Frida Kahlo, Dolores Huerta.
Anne Frank records a *diary*,
and there are Audre Lorde,
Flo Kennedy, We Wah,
Florence Lawrence,
Regina Anderson.
A horror writes *Mein Kampf*.
Fascism, and Mussolini, Stalin,
and Kuomintang China develop.

1900 to 1950

Helvitica typeface appears, as do
Existentialism, Dadaism, Surrealism,
Dali, Chagall, Miro, Georgia O'Keefe,
Mary McLeod Bethune, Morton,
Billie Holiday, Louis Armstrong,
Jack Teagarden, Sam Weiss,
Duke Ellington, Gershwin,
Huddie Ledbetter, Bartok,
Spencer, and Malinowski.
A Conference at Solvay
shakes our foundations.
Invention and discovery
bring: television, insulin,
radio astronomy, a cyclotron,
teleprinters, liquid fuel rockets, nylon,
Fermi's suggestions regarding neutrons,
deuterium, the first nuclear reaction, and
Van der Rohe builds an office at Fredrichstrasse.
Schrodinger's cat spins tales of wave mechanic's
discoveries proposing uncertainty.
Math and science explode with:
Tailleferre, Beach, Ruth Seeger,
'Flo' Kennedy, Henrietta Lacks,
Hilbert, Noether, Rosen,
Oppenheimer, Hoyle,
Alexander Friedman,
and George Lemaitre.
The meson is predicted.
Nuclear fission is described,
the Big Bang is proposed, and
spiral galaxies are seen by Hubble.
Caesium 135 enters the atmosphere
to last for 2.3 million years.

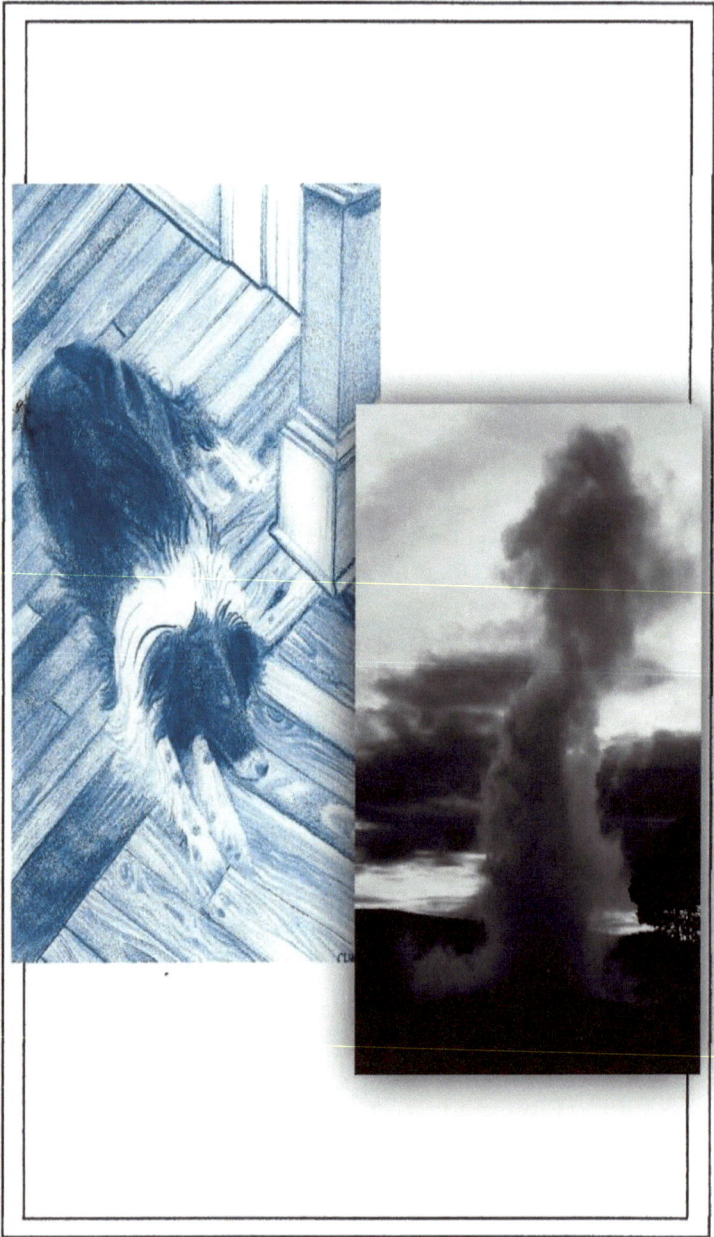

1950 to 1950 (8)

The Atlantic is flown
by Lucky Lindy in 33.5
hours with a Spirit; then
1929 begins a world wide
economic depression.
We are influenced by
Dylan Thomas, Pasternak,
Pollock, de Beauvoir, Camus,
Sartre, Emily Balch, and Demming.
Minds and souls are stretched by
Amelia Earhart, Margaret Mead,
Brecht, Forester, Hesse, Proust,
Woolfe, Pirandello, Sholokhov,
George Washington Carver,
Joyce, Kafka, T. S. Eliot,
Maria Montessori, and
Rudolph Steiner's view.
We have Graf Zeppelin,
a Volkswagen Beetle,
dehydrated food, DDT,
the Kellog-Briand Pact,
Japanese control of Asia,
and a Chinese Civil War.
Jet-powered aircraft appear, and
there is the Rockefeller center.
Christian X of Denmark
evacuatesthe entire
Jewish population
In a single act
of defiance
against
evil.

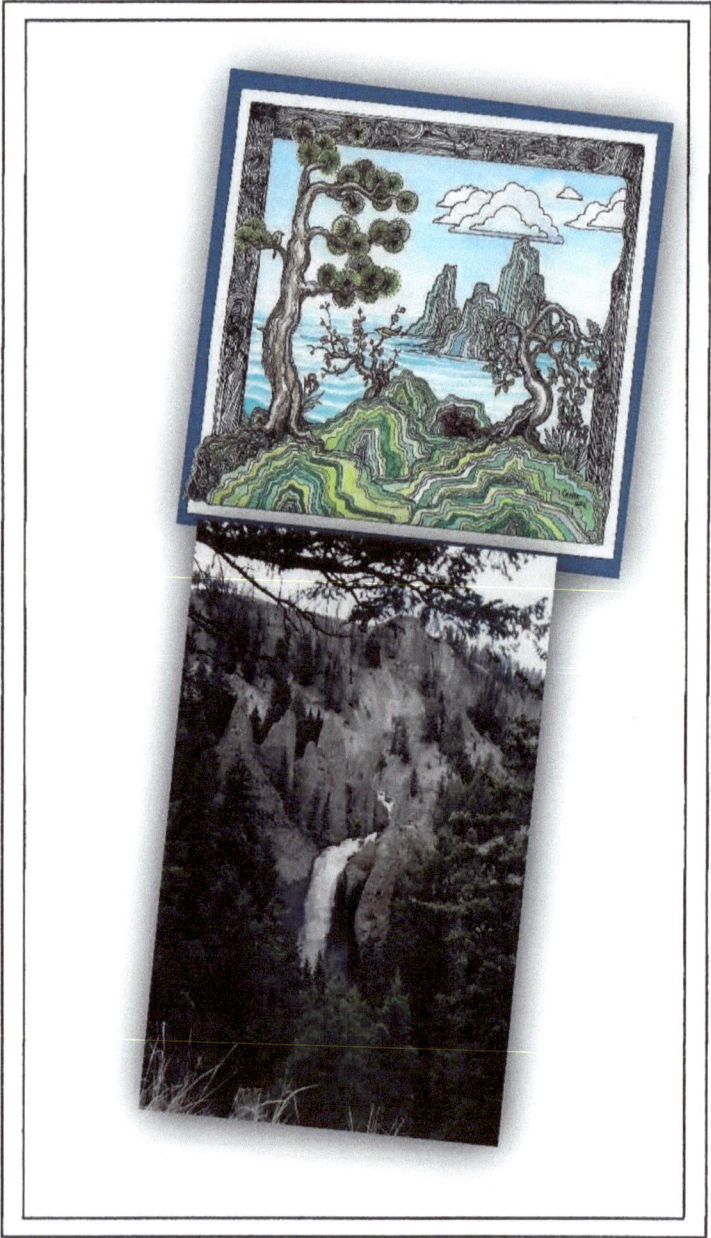

1900 to 1950 (9)

Our minds are driven by
John Maynard Keynes,
Adolf "Schicklgruber",
Mohandas K. Gandhi,
Roosevelts, Churchill,
Franco, and Chamberlain.
Franklin unwinds DNA
with Watson, and Crick
Morehi Uyeshiba draws
Aikido from the earth.
Placebo trials begin.
Neutia builds Lovell Heath House.
Women grace music with Boulanger.
Tharp and Heezen map the ocean floor.
Frank Lloyd Wright is at Falling Water.
Hollywood, and the movies grow up;
Harold Lloyd, Colbert, Fred Astaire.
George Burns and Gracie Allen.
We learn to love
Spencer Tracy, and
Katherine Hepburn,
Bogart, Bicall, Garland,
Orozco, and Riveras murals,
Olivier, Fonda, and Stewart.
Our souls learn to feast upon:
August Strindberg, Glenn Miller,
F. Scott Fitzgerald, Hemingway,
Ella Fitzgerald, Thomas Mann,
Gertrude Stein, Henry Miller,
Orwell, Huxley, O'Neill,
Tennessee Williams,
Arthur Miller, Pearl Buck,
Orson Wells, Benny Goodman,
Helen Keller, and Eleanor Roosevelt,
Steinbeck, Sandburg, and Sinclair Lewis.

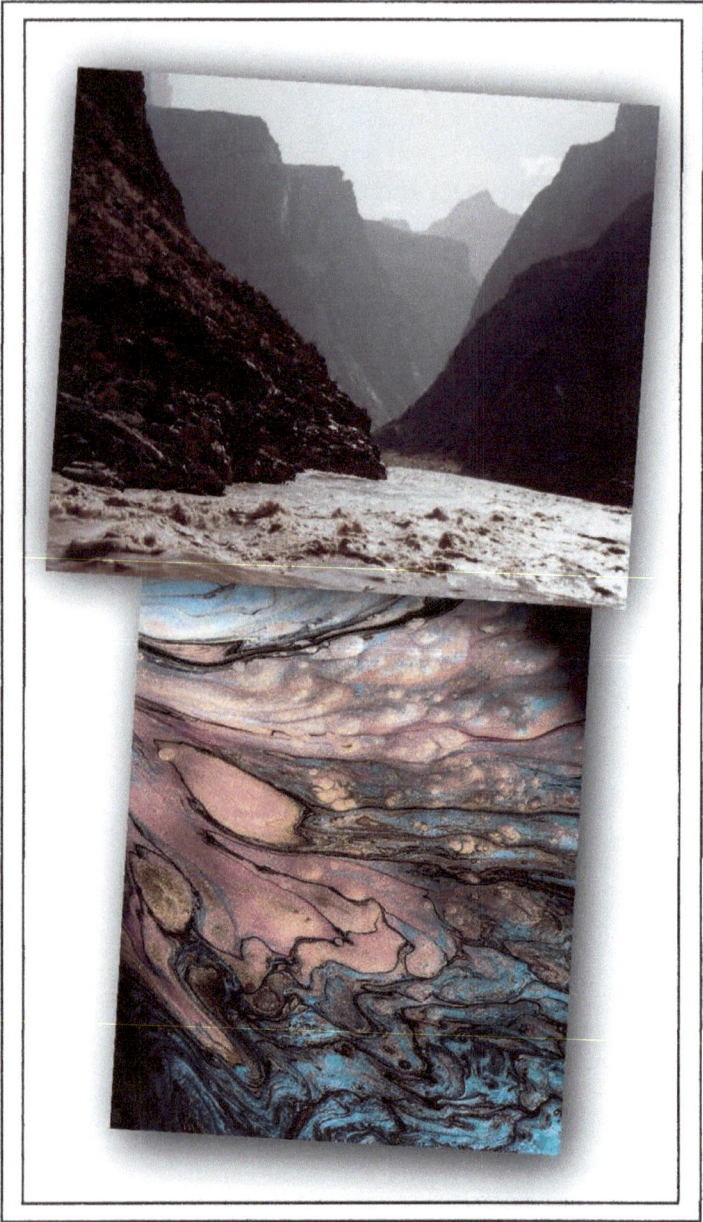

1900 to 1950 (10)

The last of Sol's planets, Pluto, is
discovered; later to be called a stolen asteroid.
d'Harnoncourt promotes native American art.
The world engages in another global war.
The Manhattan Project is initiated.
Discoveries include plutonium,
penicillin, and streptomycin.
Fermi divides an atom, and
the atomic bomb is detonated.
Other bombs are deployed against
humans at Hiroshima, and Nagasaki.
By end of war 130 million, perhaps 5%
of the human population, lay dead from
combat, genocide, and collateral damage:
V2 rockets, Coventry, Dresden, Tokyo,
nuclear madness, starvation, and illness.
We know of the poet Rabindranath Tagore.
Robert Millikan measures electron's charge.
Machu Picchu ruins are discovered by Bingham.
As Neva Boyd lays the foundations of Social Work,
she & Dagney Pederson seed modern Improvisation.
An atomic world is graced by Chadwick, Hahn, and Lise.
Philip Randolph forms the Brotherhood of Sleeping Car Porters.
Executive Order 9981, ends segregation in U.S. Armed Services.
Dame Mary Lucy Cartwright and J.E. Littlewood describe chaos.
Florence Price, 1st African American woman
composer, is played by a major orchestra.
Jacques Cousteau takes us into
the oceans with an aqualung.
Henry Wallace, and
Eugene Allen serve
the American White House.
Technological developments of war
flood the earth with newfangled things.
There is a Chapel of St. Francisco in Pampulha.
America becomes the primary world power.
From 1944 to 1956, women gain the vote,
in France, Italy, Japan, Argentina,
India, Greece, Mexico, and Egypt.

1900 to 1950 (II)

Stalin purges the Soviet Union causing
deaths estimated to be more than 20 million.
Europe is divided by a curtain coined as Iron.
A uniting of Nations is called, and chartered,
helping us sit together as NATO, and SEATO.
There is an Organization of American States.
Hutchins supports an experiment called
Chicago, at North Western University.
On Mount Palomar is a telescope;
then breaking a sound barrier,
and inventing a transistor.
Mother Theresa is here.
Mao Zedong begets a
People's Republic in China,
and in counter pose is Ho Chi Minh.
In India there are Muslim versus Hindu riots.
Beryl Markham flies Atlantic from east to west.
Burma, Pakistan, and India gain independence.
Gandhi is assassinated as he sits passively.
The Mediterranean world is redesigned
with The League of Arab States.
Indonesians and Filipinos
become independent.
Eames builds houses.
Robert Lowe, Sr. is born.
There are five Brothers Marx.
Birla Mandir Temples cross India.
Martha Graham frees formal dance.
Jacob Moreno stages Improvisation.
The French begin to falter in Indochina,
as America prepares to fall into the error.
Israel is founded, Japan recovers from war.
Abstract Impressionism appears, and we know
swing, and bebop music around the world.
The Highlander Folk School is founded
Meshima lives his life, and
the human population is
two and a half billion.

1950 to 1990

Pirelli's Building in Milan
is a prototype of the skyscraper.
'Northland' models shopping centers.
A Common Market forms in Europe.
Pelli designs the Bank in Charlotte.
In Mao's China there
is cultural revolution,
and death of 15 million.
USSR is a world power.
The International Society
of Women Airline Pilots forms
with Jackie Chocran, Jackie Parker,
Valentina Tereshkova, and Jerrie Mock.
Multinational corporations grow
world-wide integrated trade;
communication networks.
Russia deStalinized and
there are Khrushchev,
and Eisenhower.
LeCorbusier
Has built Villa Savoye,
The UN Headquarters, and
a monastery at La Tourette.
The Warsaw Pact is created.
Charles de Gaulle has France.
China develops the collective.
We celebrate Shirin Ebadi.
Cold enflames War with
Police Action in Korea,
by Nations called United.
Mt. Everest is dominated.
Brasilia is proposed by a sketch
then is created from whole cloth.

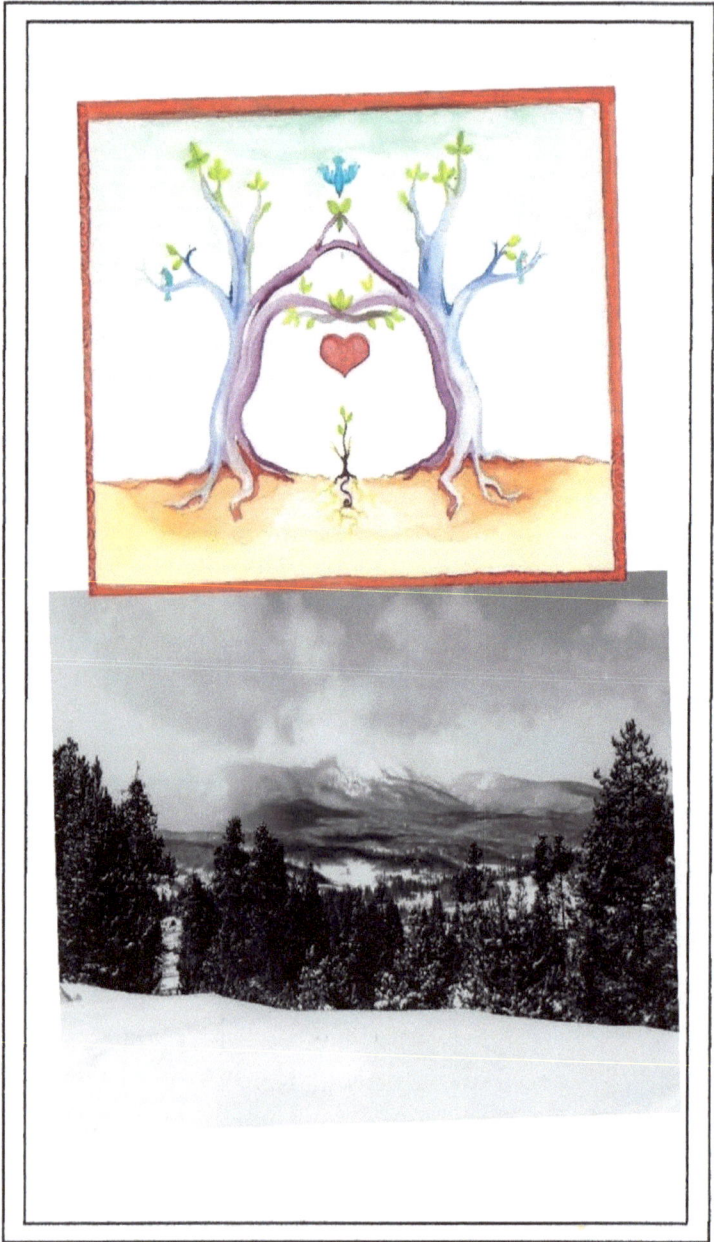

1950 to 1990 (2)

The Compass Players appear.
The Second City is founded.
South and Central America
suffer ages of dictators.
OPEC is conceived, and
a smallest atom makes
largest bang as bombs.
Semiconductor electronics make a revolution.
Pioneering the global explosion of Improvisation:
Spolin, Paul Sills, Howard Jerome, Willie Wiley,
David Shepherd, Keith Johnstone, Bernie Sahlins,
Howard Alk, Judith Greer Essex, Jonathan Glazier,
Gary Austin, Charna Halpern, Augusto Boal,
Del Close, The Committee, Jackie Lowell.
An Opera House is completed in Sydney.
Park Hill, in Sheffield, houses the poor.
We gaze up at Sputnik and Gagarin.
The AFL merges with the CIO.
Nuclear power is manifest.
Our intellect is reflected in:
Talcott Parsons, LeRoi Jones,
Hattie Alexander, Chomsky, Beckett,
Antonioni, Kurosawa, Shostakovitch,
Annie Lumpkins, Margaret Hamilton,
Virginia Apgar, Ginsberg, Ferlinghetti.
We are engaged, lifted, and changed by:
Lennon, McCartney, Harrison, and Starr,
Bob Dylan, Baez, Peter, Paul, and Mary,
Frank Hamilton, Mario Savio, folk culture.
John F. Kennedy, anti-war, and drug
revolutions shake the world. Americans
kill Americans at Kent State University.
Arms weapons are racing toward
global destruction.

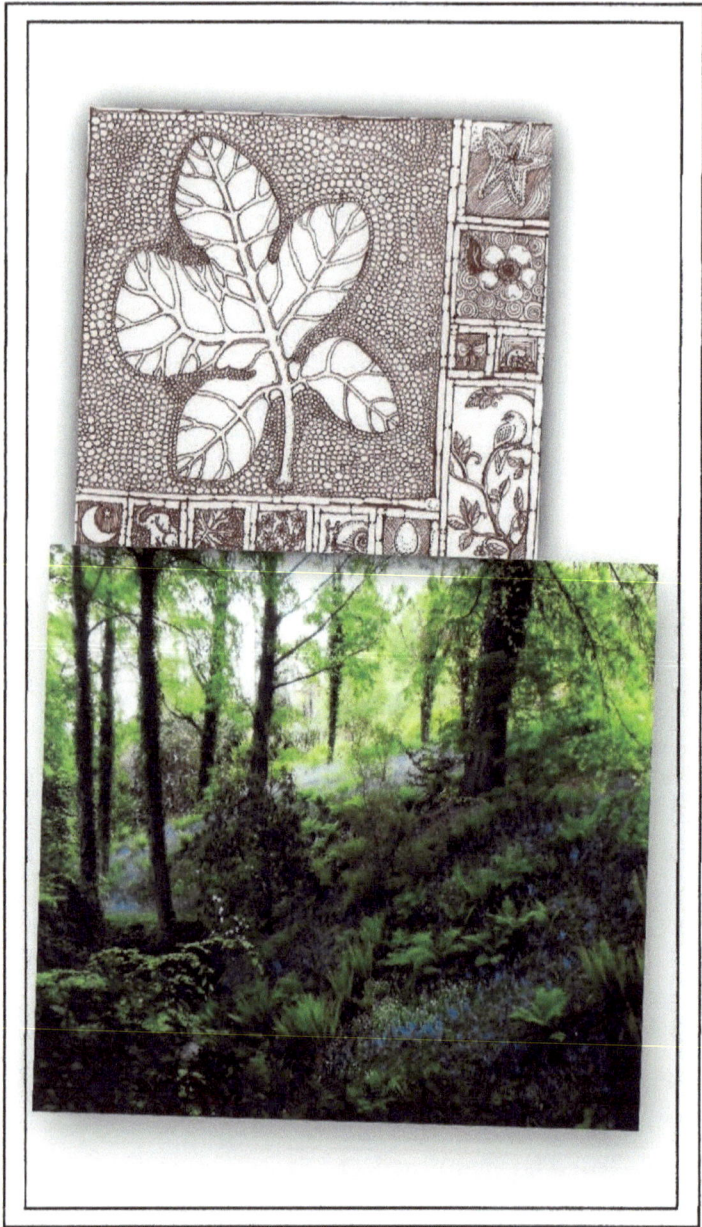

1950 to 1990

An American-Russian
crisis shoves the world to
within a day of nuclear war.
Counter-culture emerges with
Timothy Leary, Ram Das, Kesey,
Owlsley, and illegalization of LSD.
Thurgood Marshall interprets the law.
We see Chien-Shiung Wu, and Zaha Hadid.
Bernard DeKoven opens 'The Games Preserve'.
Magnetic recording, and television bloom with
Walt Disney, Red Skelton, and Ernie Kovacks.
Nkrumah wins independence for Ghana.
Bannister breaks the four-minute mile.
Africa begins decolonization. We are
beatniks, Kerouac, Cassidy, Auden,
Burroughs, Merce Cunningham,
C. Wright Mills, de Kooning,
McLuhan, Suzuki, Takaezu,
Motherwell, Charles Olson,
Black Mountain College,
William Carlos Williams,
Beaudoin, Fromm, Hume,
Neuryev and Fontaine,
Taraji Henson,
Jocelyn Bell, Ezra
Pound, and Murrow.
Rock and Roll arrives with
Chuck Berry, Haley, Fats Domino,
Sister Rosetta Tharpe, Little Richard,
Buddy Holly, and Elvis Presley.
Consciousness is expanded by
R. D. Laing, Milton Erickson,
and Paramahansa Yogananda.
Karl Popper and Thomas Kuhn
struggle over reality.

1950 to 1990 (4)

Eastern Mysticism
meets and, greets the West.
Science and technology brings:
the bathyscaph, laser light, Telstar,
electronic music, and integrated circuits.
Alaska & Hawaii become American states.
Castro, and Che Guivera shake a hemisphere.
Anna Hedgeman struggles for our civil rights.
America, engaged fully and fatally in Viet Nam.
We hear Gillespie, Basie, Coltrane, and Getz.
Oral contraceptives change everything.
Brasilia is beatified by The Cathedral.
Polio, defeated by Jonas Salk, has
Institute gracing the seascape.
Between 1960 and 1970 the
American GNP is doubled.
Women may vote in Kenya.
Women lead into space with
Mary Jackson, Dorothy Vaughn.
Japan wholly recovers, to become
a leading world economic power.
Grossman opens 'The Gate of Horn',
launching a modern folk music rebirth.
The American Civil Rights Movement sits,
stands, and walks with Rosa Parks, John Lewis,
Martin Luther King, Jr., Marian Anderson, Maya
Angelou, Andrew Young, James Baldwin, Ralph
Abernathy, Ralph Bunche, Lorraine Hansberry,
Elijah Muhammed, Colin Powell, Jessie Jackson,
Vernon Jordan, Ohey Mallock Al Shabaz.
Roe v. Wade challenges
basic American culture.
Smallpox is eradicated.
Organ transplants proliferate.

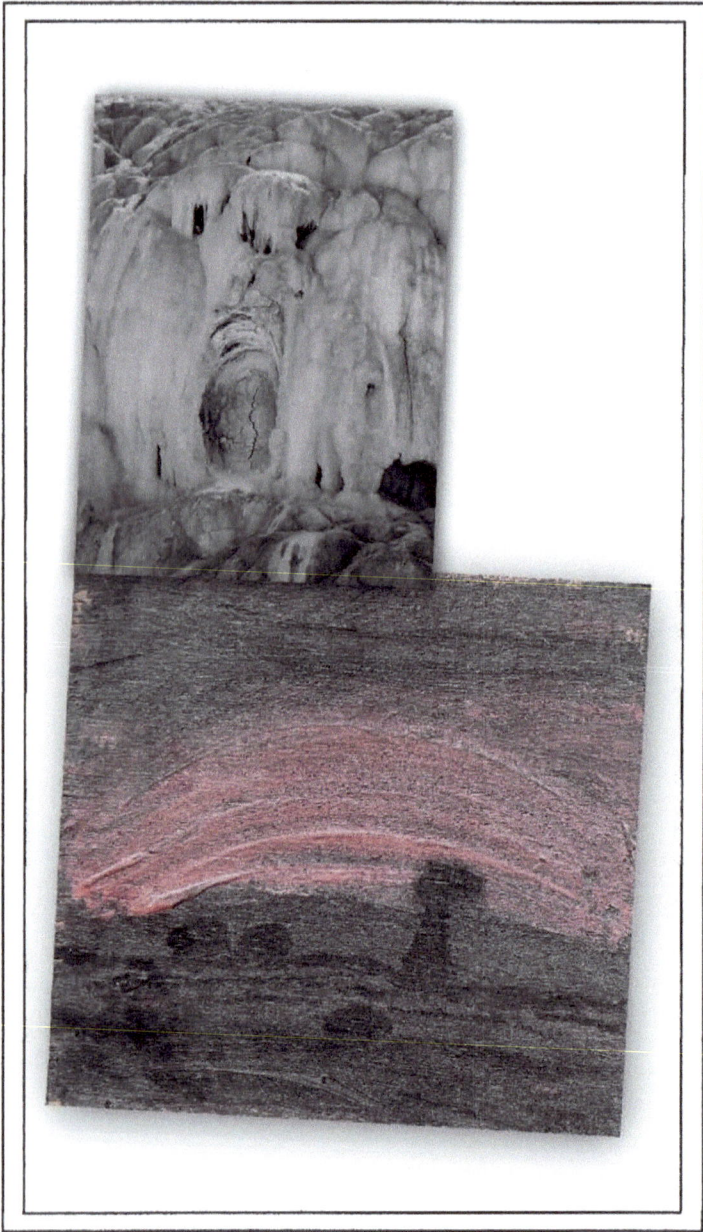

1950 to 1990 (5)

Our lives are enriched by:
Jeanne Manford, Anna Fisher,
Abzug, Solzhenitsyn, Balanchine,
Mishima, Baryshnikov, and Tharp.
We grow in the web of an internet.
Oil spills challenge the environment.
There is global expansion in sciences:
Edward Lorenz, Andrew Wiles,
Paul Erdős, Benoit Mandelbrot.
Robert Kennedy is assassinated.
Ray Tomlinson invents @, and email.
Cerf & Khan develop TCP/IP standards.
Rachel Carson sounds the *Silent Spring*.
Feminism broils, NOW is formed, and
an Equal Rights Amendment fails.
Black Panthers reinvent Eldridge
Cleaver, and H. Rap Brown, and
there is Maoism world-wide.
Taj Majal Hotel in Karachi
marks a trend in building.
We witness the human
heart transplanted.
Adorno holds forth.
Homosexuality rights
& handicapped accessibility
movements develop in the west.
Judy Chicago designs a 'Dinner Table'.
The Victoria Harbor Tunnel is completed.
English emerges as primary world language.
Leymah Ghowee, and Lee Miller grace us.
Women gain the vote in Switzerland.
American Supreme court decides
Brown v. Board of Education
changing schools forever.

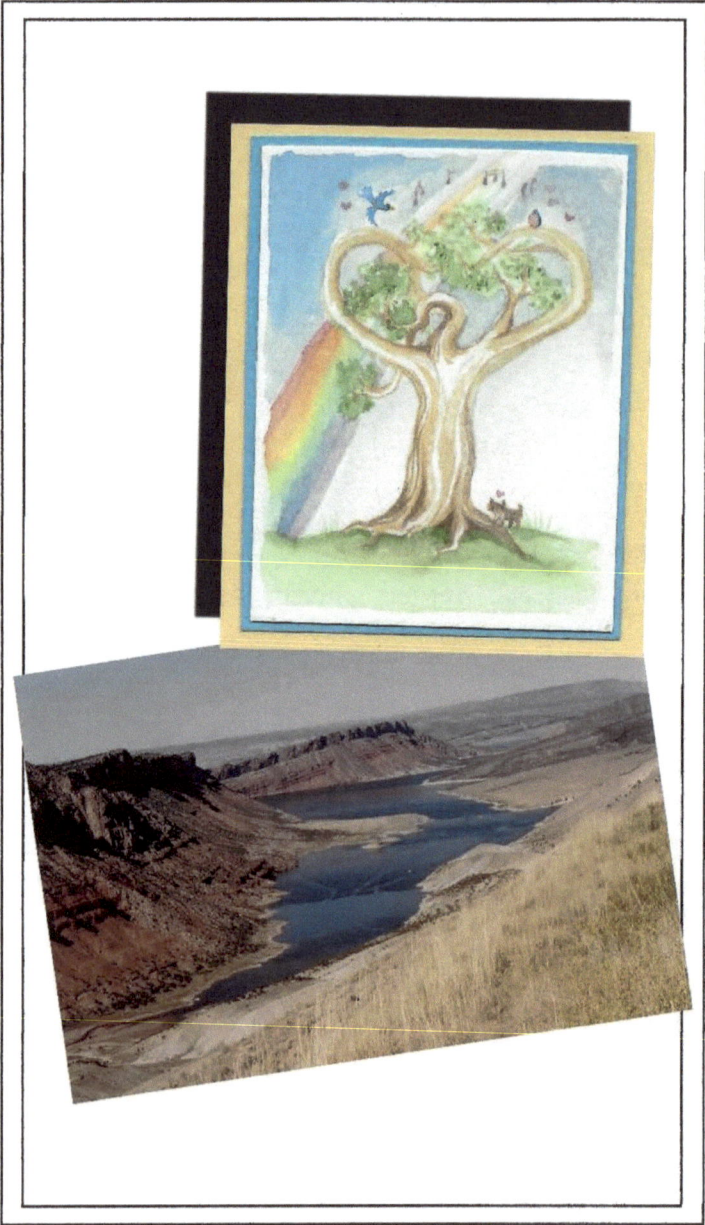

Nuclear warships, above and
below, cover the planet and oceans.
Nuclear power plants are built globally.
There are nuclear weapons test bans and
a nuclear non-proliferation movement.
The 'Third World' is coined, and
there is a world community
of 158 sovereign nations.
Quantum entangles
Gell-Mann, Bohm,
Feynman, Zellinger.
Life technologies explode.
The African continent awakes!
Small internecine wars, border skirmishes,
private wars, revolutions are world-wide.
Israel expands as a regional power
beyond six war days.
The Suez Canal closes.
NASA enters outer space.
Our minds are touched by:
C.S. Lewis, T.S. Eliot, Stoppard,
Lenny Bruce, Vonnegut, Asimov,
Habermas, Heinlin, Bradbury, Albee.
Neil Armstrong takes a step for mankind.
June Foray gives voice to Rocky & Natasha.
Voyager and Viking take to the solar system.
Oil rich countries impose global oil shortages,
while environmental crises touch everything.
Bose-Einstein condensate is a new element.
Burst of dinosaur fossil discovery begins.
Sterling designs Neve Staatsgalarie.
Louise Hay influences a new age.
Pablo Neruda is a Nobel poet.
Cirque du Solei thrills us.
Nanoscience is pioneered.
The gold standard is abandoned.
There is backlash against women,
gays, and a permissive society.
Kwanzaa is first celebrated.

1950 to 1990 (7)

Russia institutes the Gulag,
the Gang of Four are in China, and
dictatorships-collapsing worldwide.
Following a French example, the
US is humiliated in Viet Nam.
Madam Ching is arrested.
Stuart Hall speaks out.
Mars Roving begins.
3-D printing is born.
There is the first Earth Day.
We see the Baha'i Lotus Temple.
A Buddhist Komeito party is in Japan.
Union Carbide causes horror in Bhopal, India.
Concorde crosses Atlantic in 3 hours and 35 minutes,
behind the legacy of Lindbergh's crossing in 33.5 hours.
Designs by Pei, Barmon, vanEuck & Kourokawa rise.
Latin American conservative repressive regimes
first seem to prosper and are then challenged.
The Beyond War Foundation is born.
Petronas towers above Kuala Lumpur.
Foundation are laid for stem cell science.
Claud Shannon leads with digital circuits.
The Khmer Rouge kill near half the toll of
a Reich, with three million people.
Indira Gandhi is assassinated.
John Lennon is murdered.
Around the world we find
conservative parties, politics.
Indochina absorbs Communism.
In Africa there is war and famine,
drought, revolution, and independence.
Sandra Day O'Connor rises to a Supreme Court.
Benazir Bhutto is Prime Minister of Pakistan, and
Mother Teresa continues toward Sainthood.

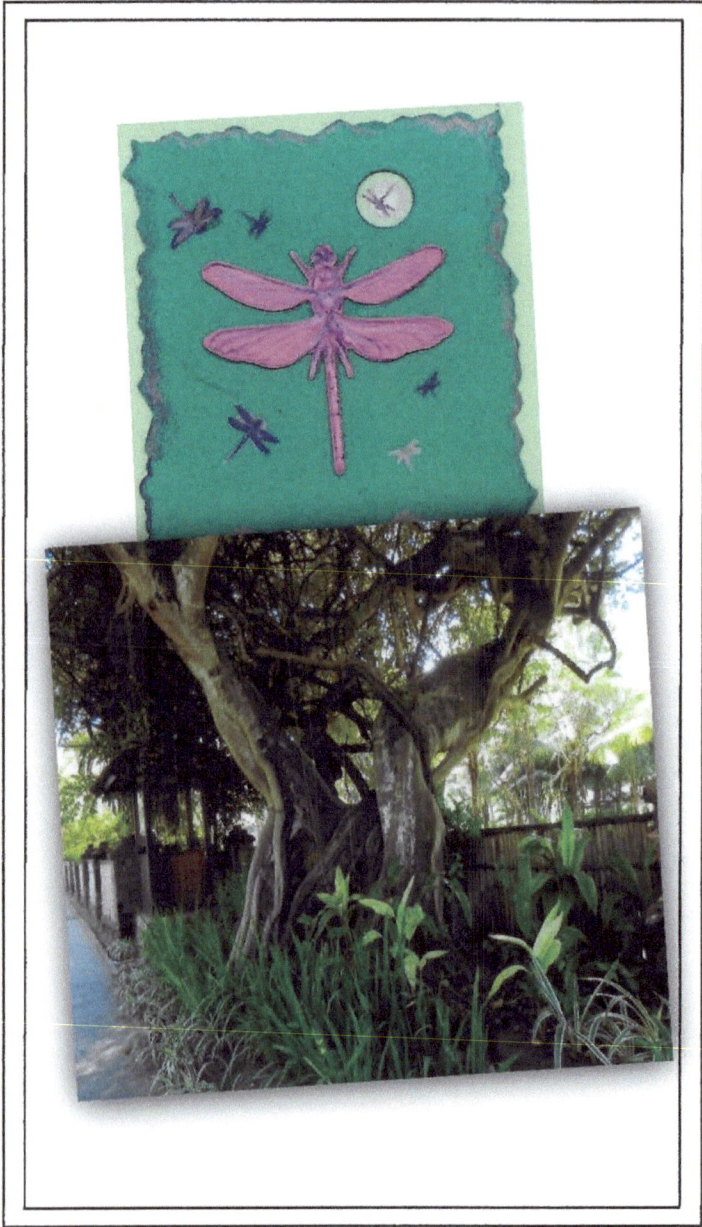

1950 to 1990 (8)

A Watergate burglary
shakes American politics.
Sally Ride; American woman in space.
Guion Bluford is first black astronaut.
The Space Shuttle 'Challenger' explodes.
Three Mile Island, and Chernobyl accidents
precipitate global anti-nuclear movements.
St. Helens, El Chichon, and Mt. Pinitubo
volcanic eruptions shake the earth.
Major earthquakes tremble Iran,
Guatemala, Mexico City,
Peru, China, and Turkey.
First in vitro fertilization.
Worldwide terrorism erupts.
Twenty-five years of Child abuse scandal
begins to rock the Catholic Church.
Women vote in Yemen in 1984.
The Suez Canal reopens.
Americans invade Panama.
Central America is in upheaval.
South Africa begins the end of Apartheid.
The music world is privileged by Gubaidulina,
Meredith, Monk, Towers, Saariaho, and Lomax.
Drugs and crack-cocaine become world problems.
There is a proliferation of sub-atomic particles.
Jonathan Michael Mawle Lowe is born. The
western European Community creates a
common market with 300 million people.
Akihito ascends the Japanese throne.
Space shuttle technology expands.
Space station Mir is launched.
Anwar Sadat is assassinated.

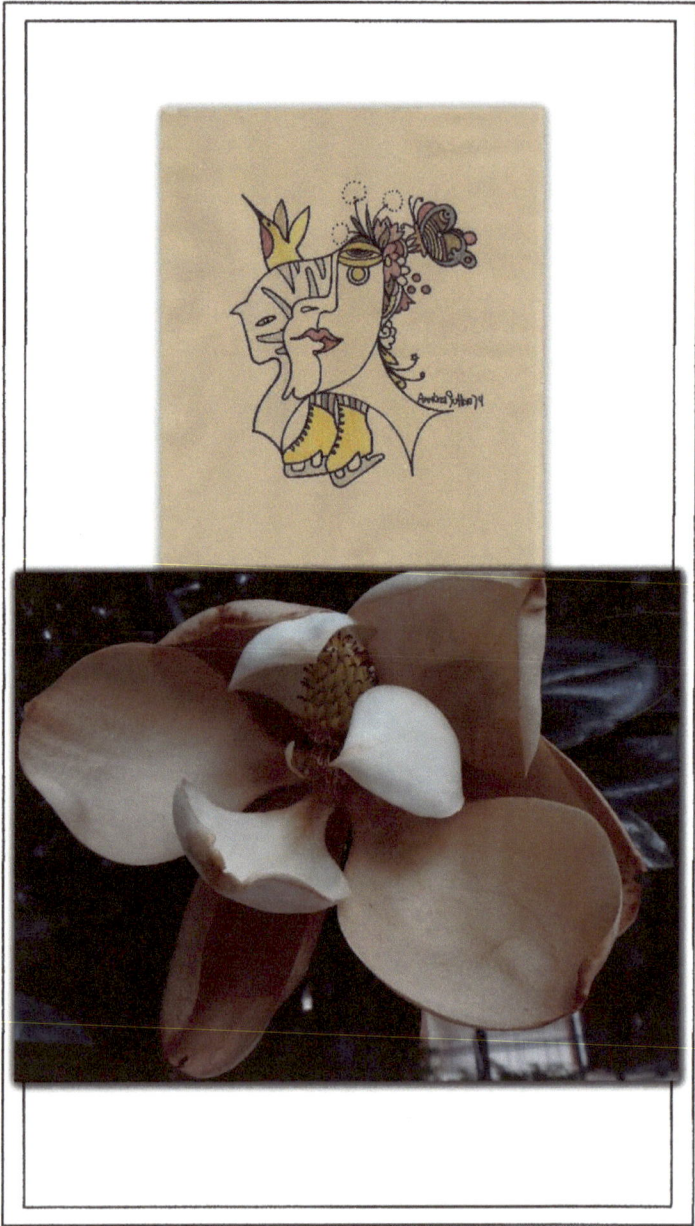

1950 to 1990 (9)

Our inventiveness brings us
FAX, video cameras, VCR,
satellite communication,
microwave technology,
and microelectronics.
Harmonic Convergence
gathers 100 million people
celebrating the reentry of the
feminine eminence on the earth.
Our politics are influenced by
Olaf Palme, Andropov,
Gorbachev, and Walesa.
A wall falls in Berlin shouting
the demise of the Soviet Union.
Ayatollah Khomeini precipitates
revolution in Iran, and then
advances Shiite Muslims.
Global food, nutrition, and
health revolutions emerge.
Technology brings cable TV,
the microchip, fiber optics, CAT,
microwave relay, Xerox copies,
and personal computers.
AIDS appears as a
world crisis.

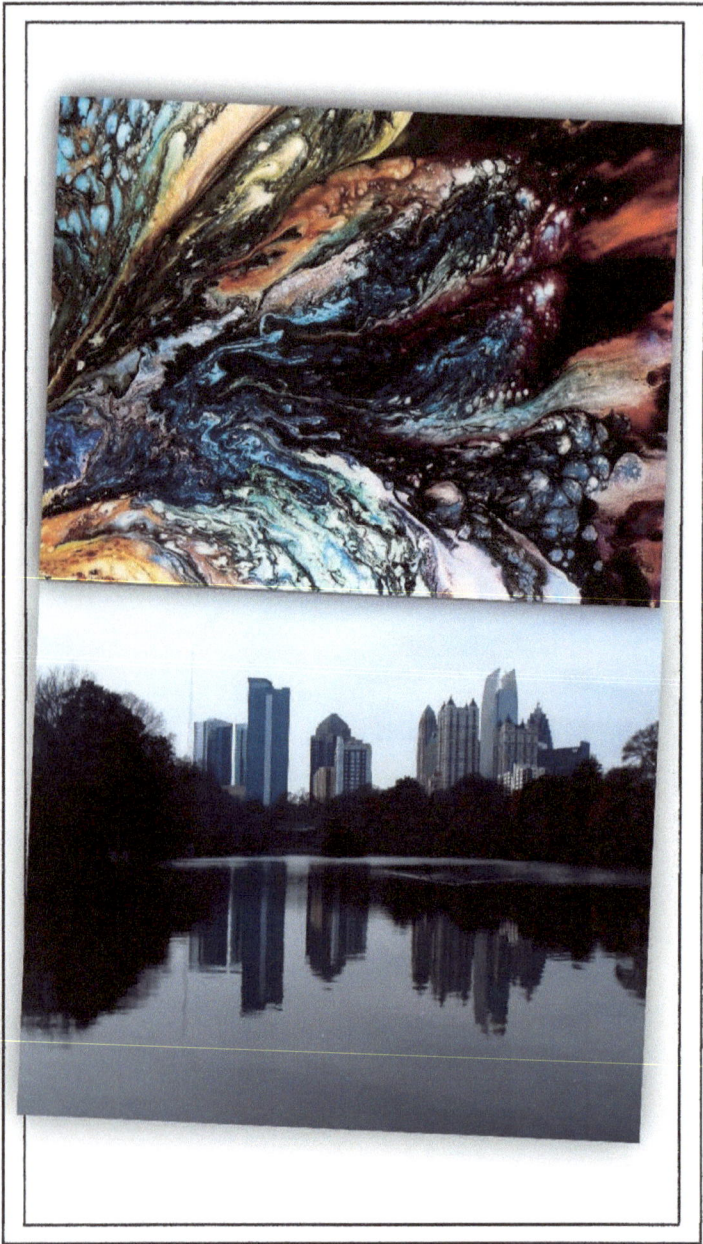

1990 to 2000

Mikhail Gorbachev receives
the Nobel Peace Prize, and
Boris Yeltsin
is the first elected
President of Russia.
The Magellan Satellite
surveys a surface of Venus.
Patricia Hill Collins talks to us.
Fay Jones designs Cooper Chapel.
There are major earthquakes in India
Los Angeles, Kobe and San Francisco.
A tunnel connects England & France.
Jemison is first black woman in space.
The Hubble Telescope is deployed
showing us the accreted planets
forming in a plane in Orion.
More hurricanes, typhoons,
floods, and draughts.
The name of Kaiser Söze enters the language.
The European Economic Community consolidates.
Building Chinese banking infrastructure commences.
There is a global expansion of improvisational Theatre.
Horner, and Schweitzer advance dinosaur science.
The first Post-WW II leadership is in place in
Russia, England, Canada,
Australia, and the USA.
The US Invades Iraq.
There are urban riots in America.
International coalitions intervene in
Somalia, Bosnia-Herzegovina, Rwanda.
In Tiananmen Square the people challenge
Chinese civil rights policy and are trampled.
Israeli-Palestinian peace efforts continue.
Pearl Bailey, and Sarah Vaughn leave.
Apartheid ends in South Africa,
a free Mandela is President.
Greta Garbo is alone at last.

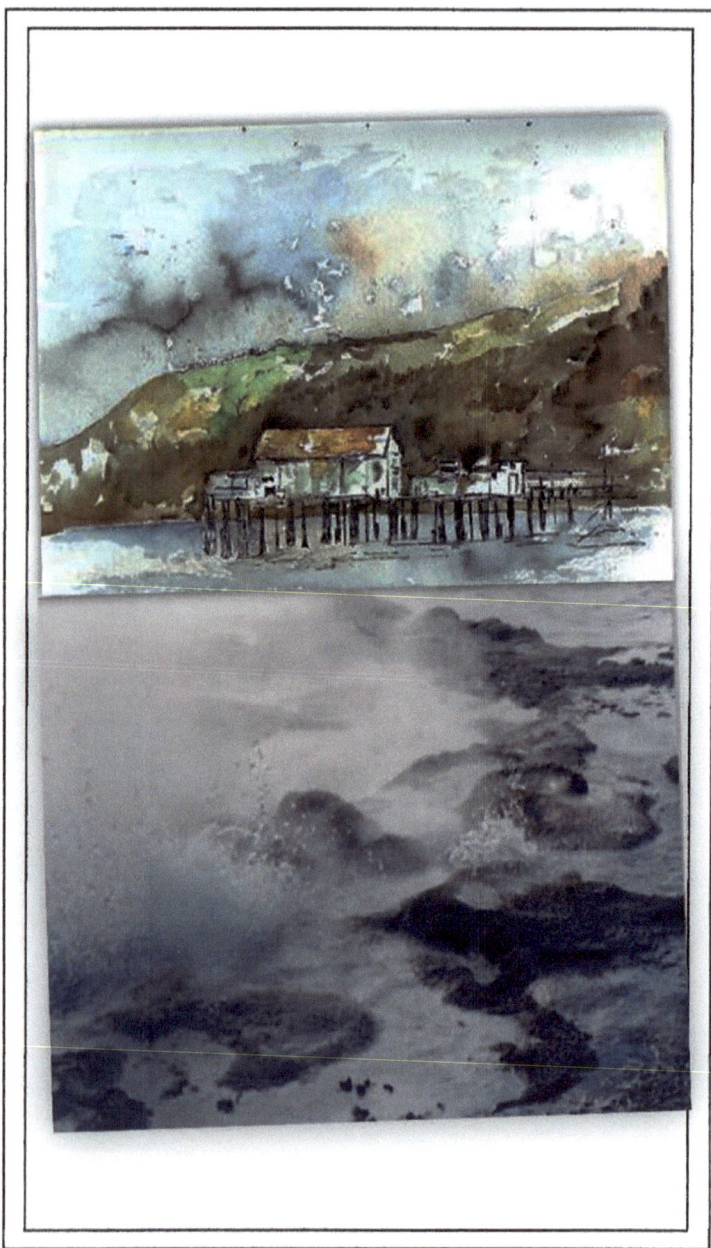

1990 to 2000 (2)

Dictatorship falls in Haiti.
America leads NAFTA, GATT.
Global networks emerge with
entertainment, movies, and
communication channels.
Info-structure develops
an Information Highway.
George Carlin makes us laugh
and cry, and laugh and cry again.
Nora Ephron directs our hearts.
The entire planet is connected by
satellite, oil, telephone, television,
fiber optics, electrical grids, radio,
cable, emergency organizations.
Gene therapy is applied to a four-year-old.
Humans develop mutual aid in the forms of:
medical groups, environmental action sets,
non-governmental service organizations,
science research teams, trade networks.
World-wide finance & shipping with
trade inter-dependencies emerge.
The IRA continues its insurgency.
Anarchy, recall from last century,
strikes the World Trade Center,
and Oklahoma City civilians.
Yitsak Rabin is assassinated.
Planets are discovered outside
our solar system and we name them,
51 Pegasi, 70 Virginis, 47 Ursal Majoris,
55 Rho Cancri Lelande 21185, and PSR 1257+12.

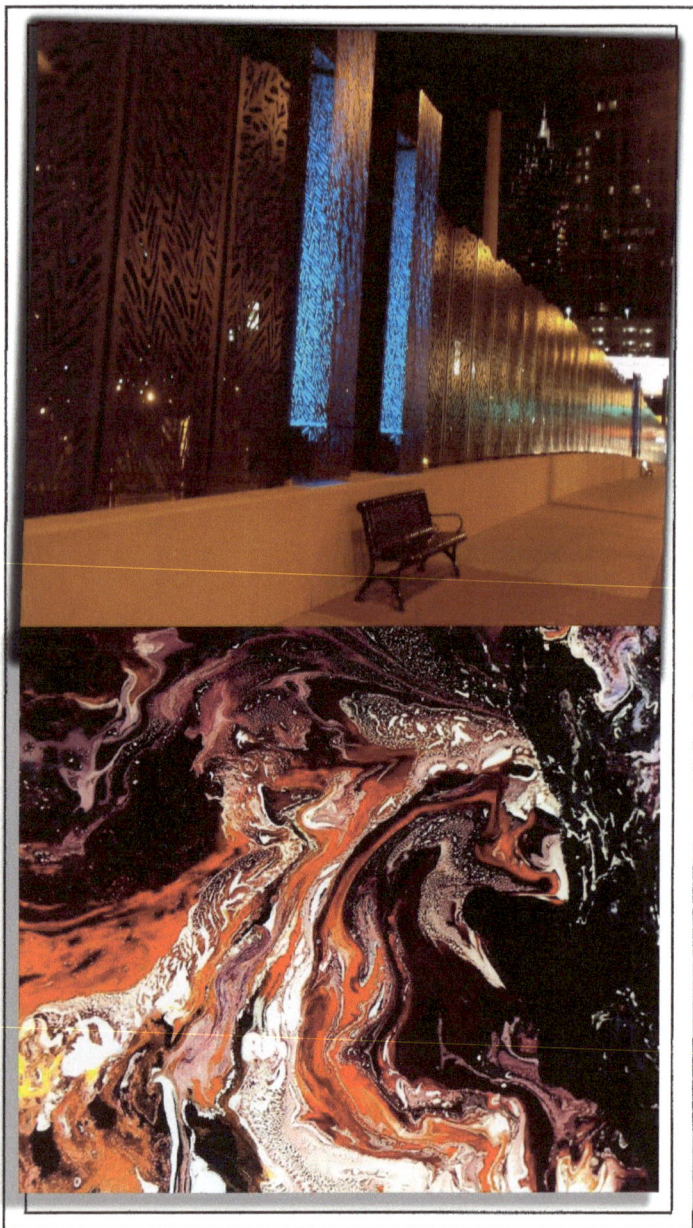

1990 to 2000 (3)

Gehry follows the Hollywood Bowl with
Guggenheim Museum in Bilbao Spain.
We call for a million men to march.
The first Earth Summit convenes.
Global communication supports growing
philosophical, and educational networks,
information and education institutions,
hospitals, water grids, air craft facilities,
and extraordinary technologies.
The UN convenes a conference;
women gathering in China.
Our planet consists of more
than 200 sovereign nations,
197 represented the 100th
anniversary of the modern
Olympic games-Atlanta;
terrorism mars the event.
Mars Pathfinder explores,
finding probable proof that
bacteriological life was there.
'Heaven's Gate' prompts suicides.
Mobutu is deposed, and Congo freed.
The US no longer
Has tallest structures,
nor largest dams,
in the world.
Eastern Europe is reorganized
with both old, and new nations.
U.S. Names Madeline Albright,
first woman Secretary of State.
There are refugees, starvation,
and war in Central Africa.
Roback, Darwish, and
Yousafzai speak
of women's
issues.

1990 to 2000 (4)

The tobacco industry admits its product is addictive,
while individual American states sue for damages.
With her only selfish act, Mother Theresa leaves
us, now more impoverished that she is gone.
Affirmative Action moves to retrograde.
Palestinians and Israelis seek peace.
Terrorism enflames abortion issues.
Business mergers break records.
Death takes Jacques Cousteau,
Viktor Frankl & Red Skelton.
Ted Turner gives one billion
dollars to United Nations.
Global warming & holes in
ozone become a major issue.
Hale-Bopp comet passes Earth.
African American WW II soldiers
receive posthumous Medals of Honor.
A Bosnian Serb convicted of war crimes.
A forced admission and apology reveals
the 'Tuskegee Study of Untreated
Syphilis in the Negro Male'.
An IBM computer defeats
a chess grand master.
Mobutu flees Zaire.
Russia joins the group of seven.
The Space Station Mir is damaged.
More trouble is in Northern Ireland.
Hong Kong is returned to Chinese Rule.
A mammal is cloned from an adult animal.
Sexual harassment develops as a world issue.
Weather made extraordinary by El Niño with
record floods, droughts, and rain forest fires.
A second American President is impeached.
Deng Xiaoping leaves China to her future.
The Akashi Kaykio suspension bridge
becomes the longest in the world.
NATO continues its expansion.
The world population exceeds
Six Billion.

2000 to 2017

A millennium
prepares for Y2K
disaster that
does not
exist.

The years
Start slowly
with more of
the same, and less
than something new,
except they say that a
human genome is now
mapped, though it is not really.

And the
movies are
even more real
than reality, like the
calculation of time itself,
and the anniversary of children
killing children is observed as though
it is somehow the natural state of things.

If business
thought it was big
it has been overshadowed
by gathering of so much that
anti-trust is a new word again to a
whole generation who did not know it
was not an old word to begin with, and there
seems to be too small a lens being used to view
these years, and decades, and millenniums, and all the
perhaps two million years that are our set of primary colors.

2000 to 2017 (2)

The Higgs Boson is detected.
Particles Accelerate at CERN.
Billions and billions of galaxies;
more than two *trillion* of them.
We see the rise of China.
Titan, open source computer
memory achieves 20 PETAFLOPS.
Miniature computer external memory
leaps from 128 megabytes to 360 terabytes.
Facebook influences human communication.
Spanish, Arab, & global youth protest in Spring.
Barak Obama becomes the 44th U.S. President.
Israeli and Mid-east regional conflicts expand.
On the back of a virus there is a radio receiver.
Nanotechnology makes the smallest, smaller.
Data bases and search engines proliferate.
Existence of tau neutrinos is confirmed.
Sexual identity tolerance is extended.
Eyjafjallajökull, and Bardarbunga
volcanos disrupt beyond Iceland.
Homo floriensiensis is discovered.
Summer Olympics host 204 nations.
Fast Radio Bursts arrive.
Tsunamis take Indonesia;
bring nuclear terror to Japan.
YouTube activates a network.
Global warming is beyond obvious.
Segue human transporter is invented.
The Gherkin building overlooks London.
The Crested Ibis is saved from extinction.
Hurricanes Sandy, and Katrina harry the U.S.
A Typhoon Yolanda devastates the Philippines.
Harold Hausen connects the human
papilloma virus with Cervical cancer.
Climate change looms.

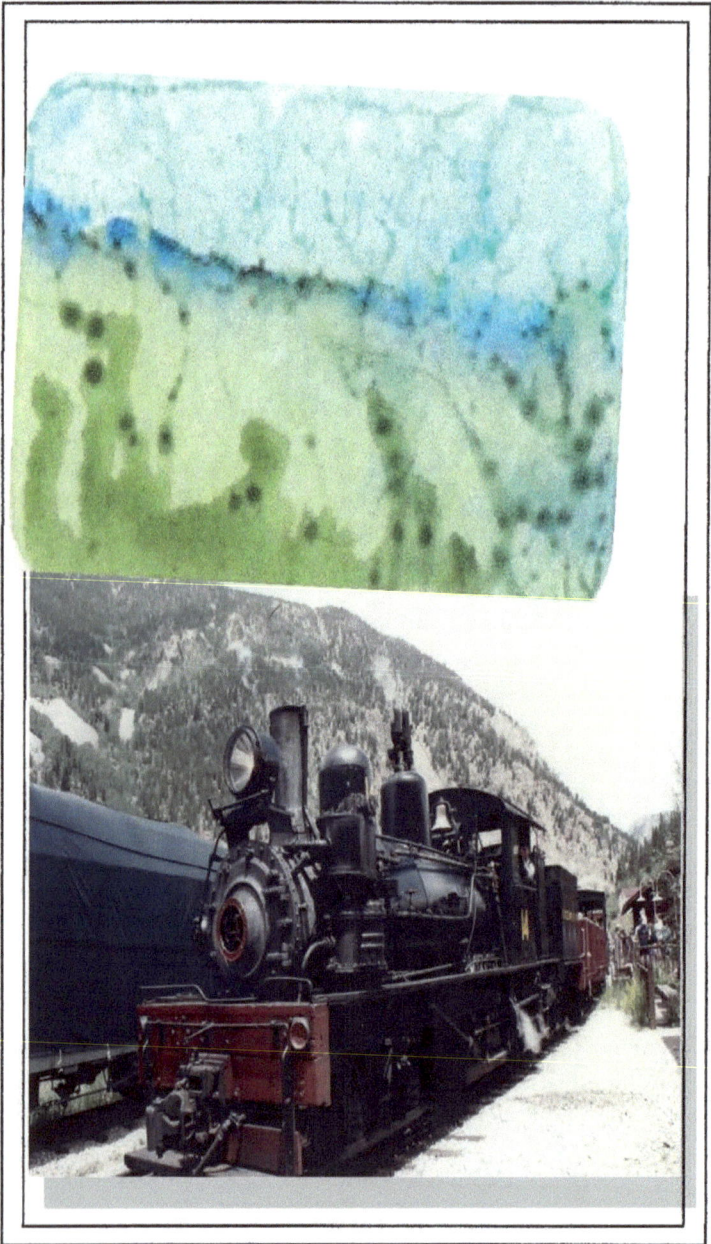

2000 to 2017 ₍₃₎

Terror attacks the U.S. again:
World Trade Center, and Pentagon.
War follows in Iraq and Afghanistan.
Youyou Tu saves millions from Malaria.
Bob Dylan receives Nobel Literature Prize.
Gun violence expands across U.S., Norway,
Tanzania, Finland, UK, Nepal, and Germany.
War visits Iraq, Afghanistan, Somalia, Chad,
Ivory Coast, Darfur, Gaza, Georgia in the U.S.
Male and female wage disparity gains attention.
'Rainmaker' harvests water out of the atmosphere.
The internet sets journalism free-ish.
We identify Gravitational waves,
Denisovan Human DNA analysis,
and synthetic Bacterial genome.
Two hundred million oil gallons
gush into the Gulf of Mexico.
Electric cars take to the road.
There are floods in Pakistan.
Drought strikes California.
The earth quakes in Haiti.
Human stem cells are cloned.
Dropleton, and Kitaev, quantum
spin liquid into new states of matter.
Innovations expand across chemistry,
physics, biology, medicine, and robotics.
YouTube becomes a universal publication.
MRI and biological spectrometry extend our view.
Stem Cell biology is used to grow parts of human hearts.
Taller than the Empire State are 24 buildings, topped by
Abraj Al-Bait Clock Tower, Shanghai Tower, & Burj Khalifa.
Inventions include the iPod, improved artificial hearts,
spray on skin gum, retinal implants, an artificial liver.
Sonoprep, permeating the skin with sound waves.

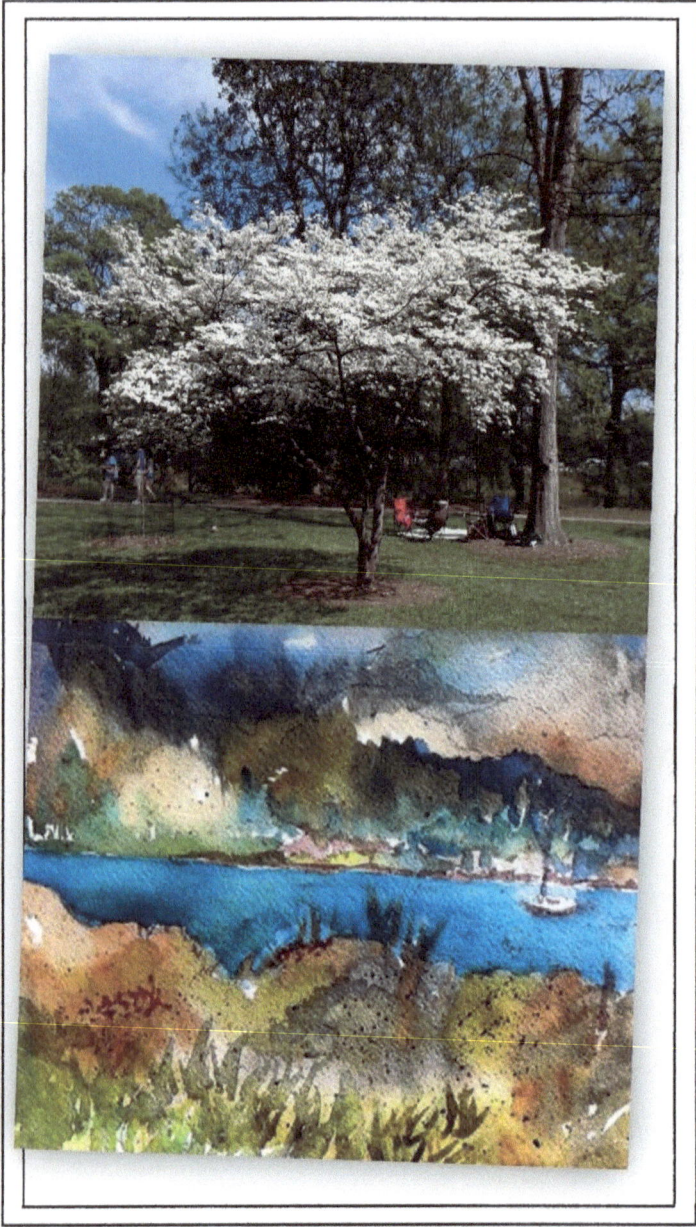

2000 to 2017 (4)

AIDS is somewhat controlled.
China climbs as a Global leader.
Now, billions, and billions of *planets*.
The Cerutti Mastodon site is discovered.
Sexual tolerance in U.S. & other countries.
Nuclear Proliferation in Iran & N. Korea.
Global Warming rises to the surface.
The Euro suffers a debt crisis.
3-D returns, remade, to film.
3-D printing is a revolution.
Francis is Pope.
'Terrorism, Turmoil, Transition'
dominate in the Middle East.
iPhone, iPad, Touch screen
surface technologies erupt.
Mass rape is in the Congo.
We see an e-book revolution.
Vuvuzelas blast their music.
Kosmoceratops is identified.
Drug wars escalate in Mexico.
Venter creates a synthetic cell.
Occupy comes to Wall Street.
Australopithecus sediba is found.

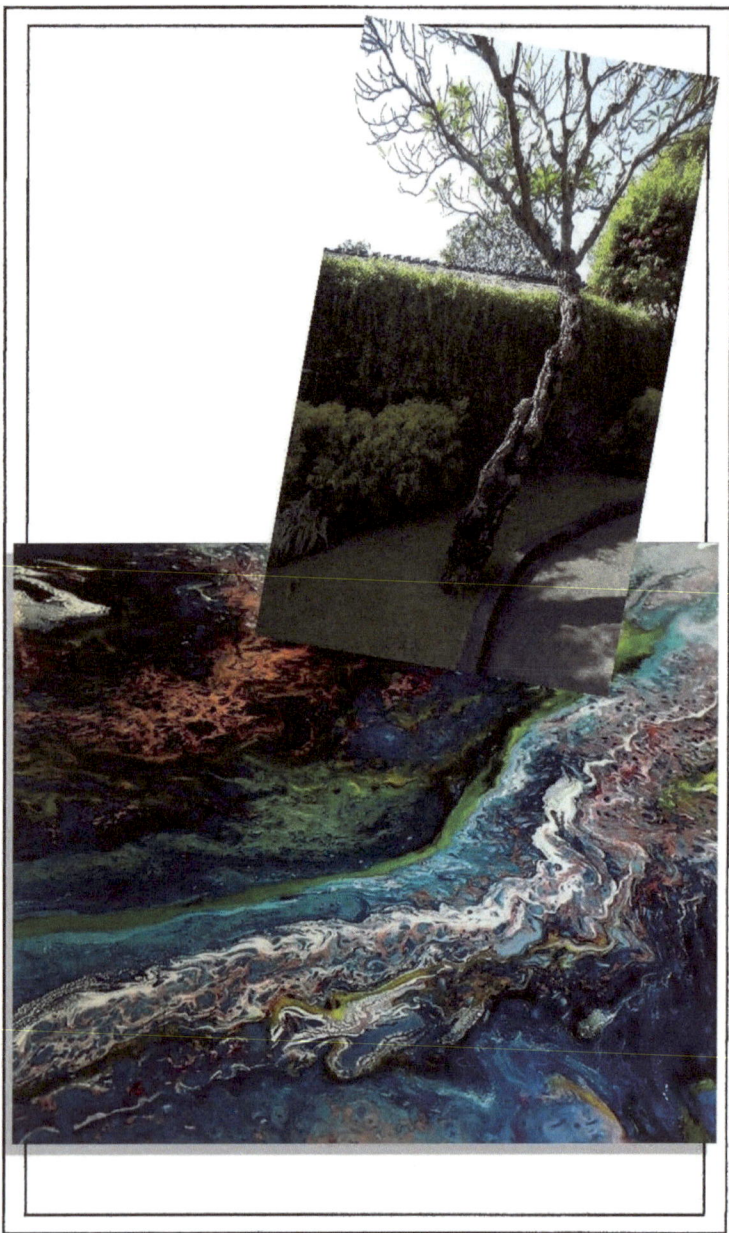

2000 to 2017 (5)

Britain votes to exit the European Union.
Rosetta spacecraft lands on a comet.
Amazon begins delivery by drone.
SpaceX lands a launch rocket.
Alzheimer's disease looms.

Mass murder continues.
Nelson Mandela leaves us.
Osama Bin Laden is removed.
New species continue to be found.
Edward Snowden leaks information.
Islamic State escalates terror and war.
Same sex marriage is legalized in U.S.

A toy car is propelled by
hydrogen extracted from water
Population of Tokyo is 38 Million.
6,000-year-old baobab is in Africa.
A tooth is used to make new eyesight.
Americans elect an incapable President.
Pando, Populus Tremuloides, tree colony;
the oldest living organism at 80,000 years.
Simone Askew is the first black woman to
command U.S. Military Academy Cadets.
Over 80 subatomic particles are listed.
More than 2,100 lives of Indigenous
people are threatened as of 2017.
The world population is
7.6 Billion.

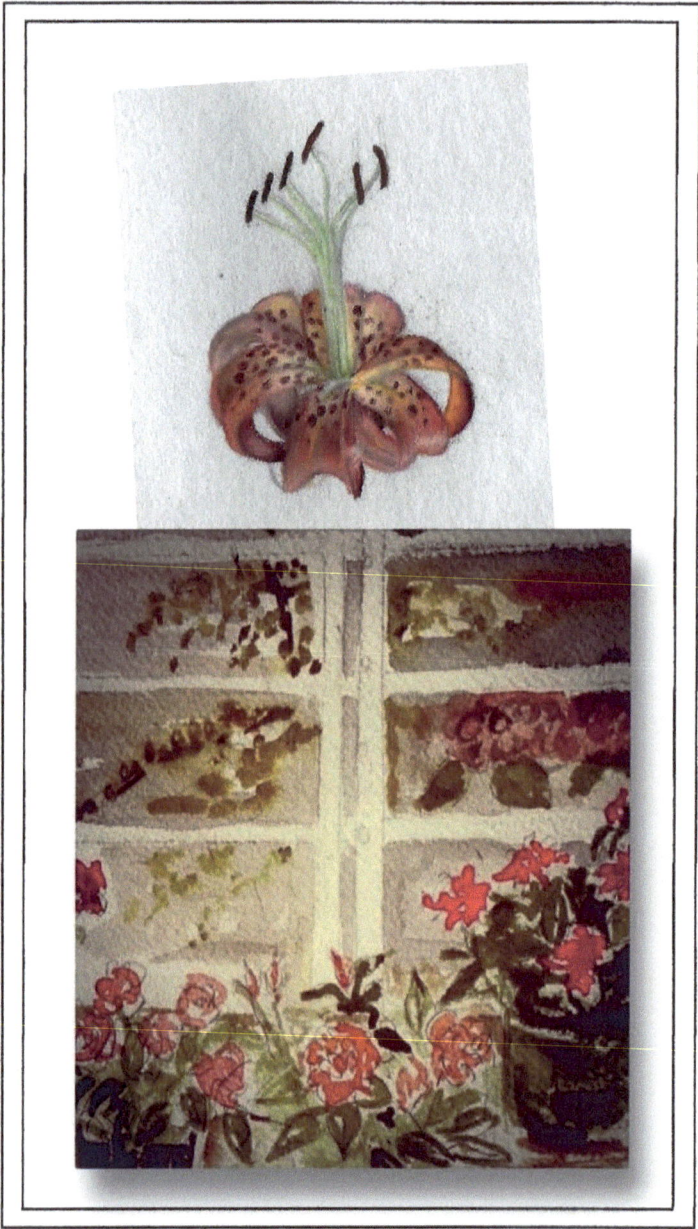

2018

At this moment humans
are the result of an un-broken
chain of evolutions and events
encompassing 15 billion years.
We are the newest co-pilots.
We are told that, "We must
be the change we wish to
know in the world".
We must become
fully conscious
of these facts
as we grow
into our
selves.

Are we doing
what must be done to
prepare for this responsibility?
We must ask, 'What are we doing now
to attend to the further development:
physical, mental, emotional,
personal, family, spiritual,
and metaphysical being?
What am I doing today
to become a more full
member of our truly
global community?
I know we can.
As I look over it all,
I hear Steinbeck saying,
"Some bad ones there are
surely, but by far the
greater number
are very good".

How *The Greater Number* Came to Be

In 1988 the state of the world had been leading me into a depression
of the spirit. Social, and economic promises from the cultural
revolution of the 1960s and 1970s seemed to have faded into
"the more things stayed the same"; the future looking bleak
at best. Our child, was due to be born later in the year
and would arrive as Jonathan Michael Mawle Lowe,
Deeper musing led me to think of the beginning of human
writing, near 4000 BCE, by count of the Gregorian calendar.[1]
The questions came asking what happened between
that event and what after another six millennia?
Listing things produced a great number of people, events, items,
cultures, oddities, and general matters that fit into that first thousand
years. This went on until nothing more came to mind. Next was the
same question regarding the following thousand years, then the
next, and the next. For hours, and then days, I moved back
and forth through the early millennia adding new
thoughts, expanding the edges of my thinking.
As the ideas grew, there came the new era, now called Current (CE), and
the creation of time frames of two hundred years each, until the sheer
volume of available data prompted me to make some time frames
shorter, starting in 1800. By the end of the first week the scribbled
pages were filled with more good things than I could
have hoped for, and my spirit was lifted.
A guiding format developed that the entries would be brief, and
Would fit into general time frames, with reference to chronology.
For months, years, and then three decades I added items as they came
from my life, thoughts, conversations, reading, study, and research,
observation, theatre, dance, television, movies, radio, and chance
encounters. By 1996 there were 25 typed pages, block printed and
filled with things that we had been, done, created, discovered or
stumbled into. A dear friend said that it was fascinating,
yet it was so dense that it was difficult to take in.

Inspiration!   'CTRL/A/CENTER'

The words stuttered, and sputter and rolled into 40 pages of
what looked like extended poetry. I began calling it my Time Poem.

---

[1] By some calculations, using December 25th to January 20th as arbitrary dates for
the beginning of the change to Anno Domini, the Hebrew calendar gives us the
date of 23 Tevet, 3762 as the beginning of the written word.

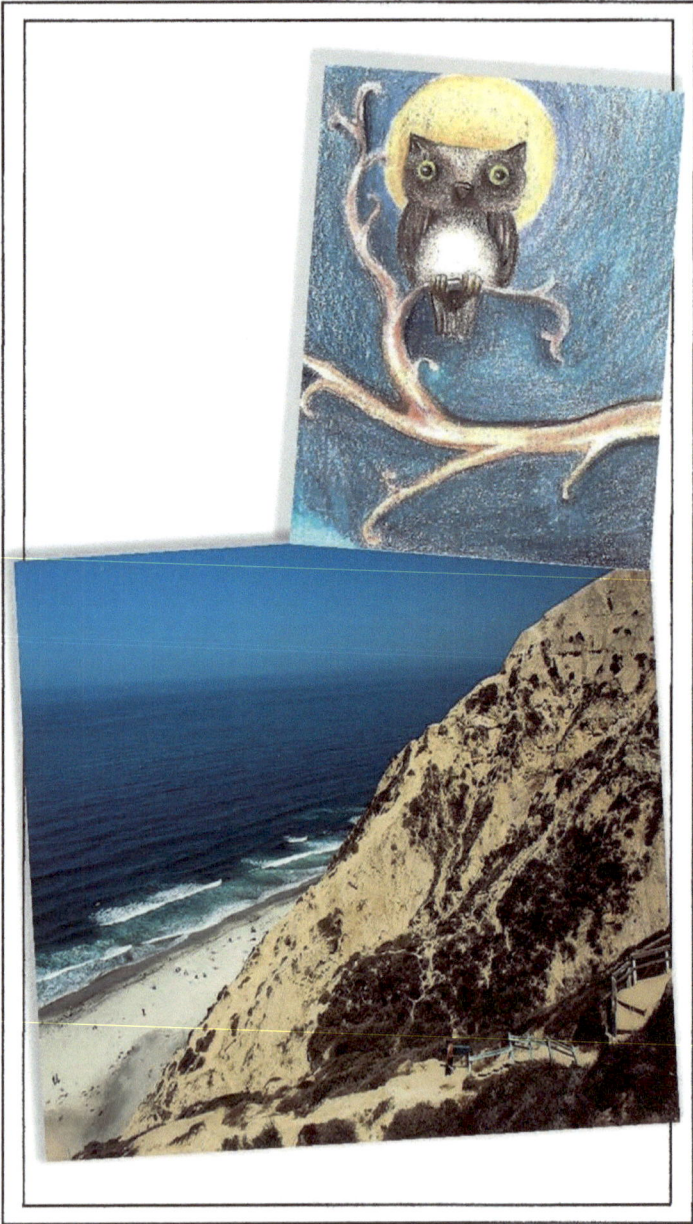

How *The Greater Number* Came to Be (2)

The first external reference work consulted was an almanac.
It provided discoveries beyond time sets. Wonders like
carbon, gold, and mercury were noted as having
been discovered simply sometime during 'BC'.
There were also many references to things of which I was aware
that had not yet come to mind. A Christmas gift of a large history
timeline book started my first real dive into details of dates,
cultures, creations, and events in our miracle called time.
An important guideline developed that I could not make an entry of
anything with which I was not at least a little familiar. If it were to be
in my Time Poem, learning something about basics was required.
Next came a long look at the histories, and stories of women in our
world, inspired by Seneca Falls, New York where I first read, The
Declaration of Sentiments (and Rights), carved into a
great wall at the Women's Rights National Historic Park.
My hands eventually came upon a giant of a book, foundational
in the history of architecture.[2] More than a year was spent exploring
Sir Fletcher Banister. A leading insight of many architects and builders
was that buildings and their traces are our footprints on the planet.
In time it became apparent that the record being gathered had my own
Euro-centric bias. This sent me into deeper investigations of
cultures, people, and events in other parts of our world.
It also came with the reality that all the great libraries
together cannot provide more than a glimpse of it all.
An overview began to grow from a story told of a great dome,
covered on the inside with identical, perfect pearls.
In each pearl, the entire dome can be seen;
the ocean visible in a drop of water;
all of life in a single cell.
In 2001 a friend showed my Time Poem to the great photographer,
George T. Henry, honored in, *A Sesquicentennial Look Through 50 Years
of George Henry Photography, Coe College*, and author of four books
featuring his life, and photographic genius.[3]
A lovely Easter visit with his warm family gave me the chance
to learn that his photography portfolio was beyond extraordinary.

---

[2] *Sir Richard Banister's A History of Architecture*, 20th Edition, edited by Dan Cruickshank.
There are no direct quotes from this work.
[3] See page 229 for specific references to George's book

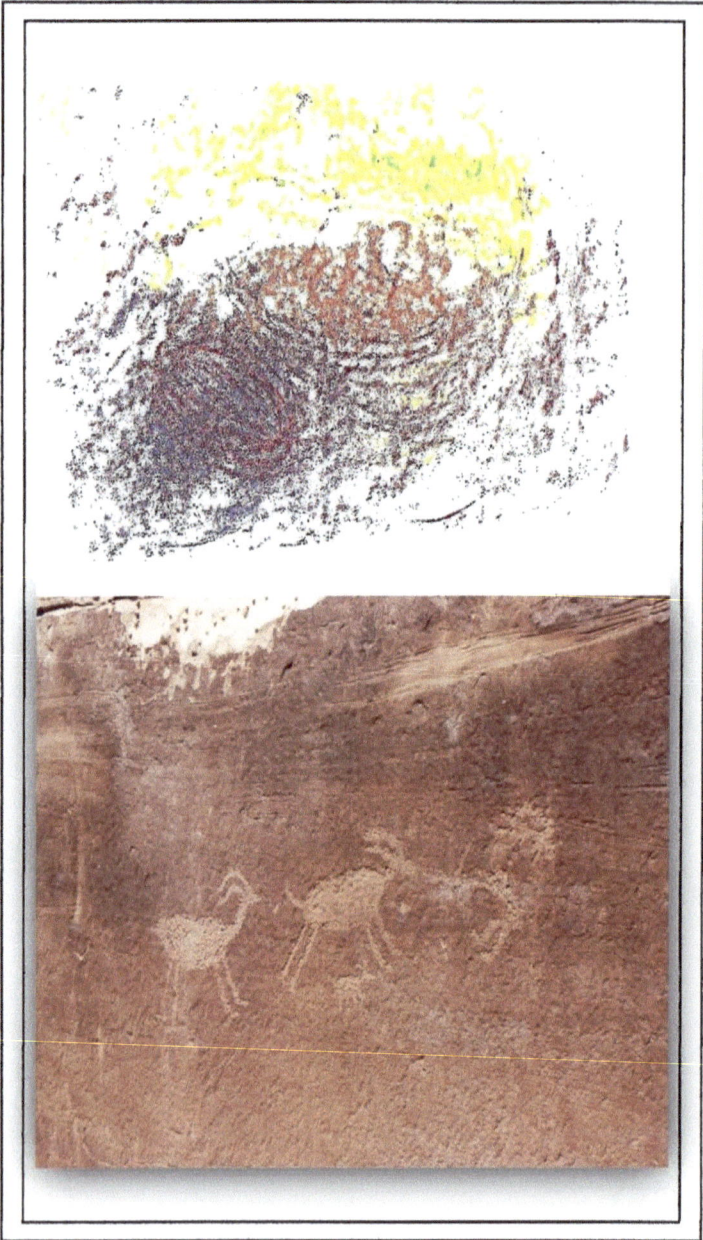

How *The Greater Number* Came to Be (3)

My Impression was that rather than merely looking at pictures
he had taken, it was as though I were seeing through
his eyes, and experiencing his vision and emotion.
We talked about the meaning and purpose of our
work. By that time my poem had been named
The Greater Number, from the Steinbeck quote.
A few weeks later I received a stack of three by five photographs; more
than pictures that reflected data, he had engaged the shapes of the
presentations of the words, and the heart of what were then
named my *Word Forms*. George's artistry added a
sumptuous new depth to the exploration.
The photos also presented the seemingly impossible task of
matching them with the *Word Forms* requiring using a frame of mind
from Improvisation.[4] Over the course of a week, while riding a bus to my
work, I entered the state called "Impro", and continuously blind shuffled
the pictures together, after which I virtually tossed them into the then
78 pages of words. By kismet the photographs landed where they each
reflected, enhanced, embellished, and gave a somewhat divine support
in impressions revealed by the juxtaposition. George suggested that
we needed something more than blank white background
for the photography.
Crysta Rosella Luke is an exceptional artist from Stone Mountain,
Georgia, USA. She came to know, and to be charmed by the positive
nature, the shapes, and the delightful photography of *The Greater Number*.
We talked about the idea of creating some border to frame the photos.
After a while she returned and said that she could not think of anything
that would work for my purpose. Instead, perhaps her artwork could be
somehow useful. She offered sketches, and fine art produced during the
eight years of work from the age of 16. She was 24 at the time. Crysta
said I could use whatever might be of value. It was a dazzling offer.
Integrating the words, and the photographs re- produced
the dilemma of how to place the work. Improvisation
to the rescue, with shuffling and tossing into pages.
Her deep, capricious, delightful, and gifted
artistry produced an aura of wonder.

[4] The state of mind came from my work in the then emerging field of Applied
Improvisation. *Improvisation, Inc.: Harnessing Spontaneity to Engage People and Groups*,
San Francisco, Jossey-Bass/Pfeiffer, 2000 (Updated as *Improvisation, Inc. Revised
Edition 2017: An Applied Improvisation Handbook. Atlanta, GA, RLJ Publications, 2017.*)

How *The Greater Number* Came to Be (4)

Just as the photos had fit the *Word Forms*, the works of art extended beyond the forms of the words, and beauty of the images.
Her artistic vision offered a whimsical,
and spiritual subtext to the project.
As the book grew, there came a need for more photography, and I began to add my own, which also created the need for more works of art.
Patricia Ryan Madson is a renowned Improvisation pioneer: Emerita, Stanford University, founder of the Stanford Improvisers, The SIMPS, and author of one of the great books on the advancement of Improvisation, beyond the theatre, and comedy.[5] She is also a superb water color artist who gathers light and color, into love and compassion.
When asked if she would contribute to *The Greater Number*, she graciously offered her work without limit. Her 'Improv Wisdom' and artistry gave space and time that fully engages the whole work.
Recently, a high school friend of my now grown son has surfaced as a startling artist, pioneering a stunning, and unique abstract expressionist school, calling on a psychedelic fusion, of color, materials, images, world views, and emotions.
When I asked if she might be willing to add her art to *The Greater Number*, she also made everything available, and offered whatever I might wish to use. Another stunning offer. The light which shines from her work cast a vivid glow on our growing collaboration.
Included in the mix are two entries by my son as a child, and two precious pieces given to me by dear friends from the past. The result is that this Time Poem, this *Word Form*, this labor of love, attempting to capture "A glimpse of our universe and sort of everything in it", is a concert played by eight exceptional artists, representing five generations, and an age span of 119 years.
A year was spent in a Google search of every entry, to verify dates, names, spelling, and details. The result included unexpected treasures. Where the entry was Li Poe it verified the dates, and was accompanied by examples of his poetry. The same with Monet's paintings, and more. Details of the science, and stories of the people, opened to me.
I came to realize that part of the purpose of this book is to challenge readers to search for more from references which are not familiar.

---

[5] *IMPROV WISDOM: Don't Prepare, Just Show Up*. New York, NY, Bell Tower, an imprint of the Crown Publishing Group, a division of Random House, Inc., 2005

How *The Greater Number* Came to Be (5)

You will discover various personal, and arbitrary decisions regarding grammatical choices, and punctuation that were required to facilitate, clarity, shaping the forms, and in helping the visibility of the ideas. The first image pages had been the product of simple cutting, and pasting. Later came some Photoshop shading that made them appear to be lifted from the surface.

A design element in this book uses aspects of cognitive dissonance. Our brains expect to see things in familiar relationships to one another, and we seek the repetition of patterns. In general, sets of pictures are expected to be in parallel within a frame, and perpendicular to one another. They are also usually expected to be completely within their frames, where further relationship repetition is generally a beacon of order. Shading patterns should be consistent. Images, and words usually have intended relationship in meaning.

In *The Greater Number* there are purposeful, and especially random disruptions of such patterns. In the face of simulated chaos, the brain experiences stages of re-orientation, and reorganization at higher levels of consciousness. This can result in confusion, or can be very like re-booting a computer by shutting it down, in preparation of changing operating systems. At the highest levels, deep alterations of consciousness may be achieved.

Waterfalls flow into abstractions; fishing poles and oceans share wave patterns. Final relationships were done using Photoshop to adjust size. The state of 'Impro' aided placement. No photographs, nor works of art have been photoshopped.

At a point it was necessary to create a beginning and an end to our journey. The fantasia of our universal beginning, advent and appearance of life, and of a great tribal period of unrecorded human time, served this purpose, along with a general personalization, in terms of my own family, and our particular time, providing a grounding perspective. Finally, there is the challenge for us all as we continue on this living journey, taking control of the forces of our universe, taking the matters of life off automatic pilot, and into our own hands. The challenge begins with allowing for a change of attitude as Lennie Ravitch advises in *Everlasting Optimism: 9 Principles for Success, Happiness and Powerful Relationships*, Tel Aviv, 2017.

Acknowledgements

As always, there is thanks to God in all her forms, all his majesty, and all their wonder, for making everything possible. My son, Jonathan, allows everything in my universe to make sense. He has also been present since the birth of *The Greater Number*, and as he has grown and matured, and his comments, and appreciation have been woven into it, as they have been integrated into my life.
This work has been 30 years in the making, and so thanks are truly due to all who passed into, and some out of, my journey during this time. The life and wonder of Vernon S. Cox expanded my perception of the universe beyond measure, along with Aikido and Improvisation. The people of 'The Beyond War Foundation' (changed to The 'Foundation for Global Community', and then retired), and the philosophy of the organization swayed my thinking, and feeling of new orders of understanding which transcends local universe. They led me to Sister Miriam MacGillis, whose world view inspired my journey into the possibility of a truly positive outlook, based in fact. Her vision ultimately led to the challenge of *The Greater Number*. A host of teachers of wisdoms alternate to my upbringing, have offered more than can be spoken of in words. Among them are: *Maharishi Mahish Yogi*[1], Baba Gi, *Baghavan Sri Sathya Sai Baba*, among Some people were part of the specific evolution of *The Greater Number*. Susan Lovitch is the lovely woman who said it was interesting yet so very dense, and thus opened the portal to this glimpse. Jan Roelofs introduced the 'time poem' to George Henry. She also has been selfless with gifts of professional, spiritual, and emotional support. Crysta Rosella Luke, and George Henry are co-creators. Beyond their participation with the highest levels of artistry, and understanding, the way each embraces the scope and beauty of life adds a unique delight to the work in which we have been engaged. Their presence on the earth would have been enough. The great hearts, and souls of Patricia Ryan Madson, and Sophia Sabsowitz, as much as their lovely fine art, led me to include their work which has added such depth and wonder.

---

[1] Names in italics are those of dear ones who have passed on from this plane of life.

Acknowledgements (2)

Herman Davis taught me the basics of PhotoShop,
which has allowed me to place the artwork and
photography in interesting juxtapositions.
The creative and talented people in the Atlanta,
Georgia, and world Improvisation communities
who have touched my life are legion. They include
Parents and students at Arbor Montessori School, at
The Atlanta International School, and the theatre, and
Improvisation students at Oglethorpe University, Atlanta,
Georgia have moved me to perpetual states of wonder,
and delight in our delicious universe.
There are so many others to name, yet so many
added light and joy and respect and honor and vision
and purpose and laughter and interest to my life; they must
know they have my grateful thanks. Perhaps some will think of the
times our paths crossed with smiles, and stories of our days. I must
also say thanks to a group of my son's friends who have given me
immense joy. They include: Travis Verner, Joseph Thomas, Davis
Herman, Ben and Kait Tracy, Asher Rayis, Niko Hawley-Weld,
Rachel Ramsey, Laura Aguayo, Rachael Busey, Shiva Rouhani,
Celine Mollet- Saint Benoit, Charles Vanijcharoenkarn,
Rohan Zhou-Lee, Nik and Tanya Beisert (née Lancaster),
and Joann C.S. Smith.

Credits for the Sweet Images

George T. Henry– Photographer {78}

George Henry has been the official photographer for Coe College,
Cedar Rapids, Iowa, for half a century. As an exquisite
photographer he was honored with the book *Coe*
College: A Sesquicentennial Look Through
50 Years of George Henry Photography.
Row Away from the Rocks is the story,
with his photography, of a 40 year
career as a whitewater boatman.
https://www.clir.org/hiddencollections/registry/hc.0874

Pages: 10, 12, 14, 22, 24, 26, 28, 34, 36, 38, 40, 42, 44, 46, 50, 52, 54, 56, 58, 60,
62, 64, 66, 68, 70, 72, 74, 76, 78, 82, 84, 86, 88, 90, 94, 96, 98, 100, 104, 106,
108, 110, 112, 116, 118, 122, 126, 128, 130, 134, 138, 140, 142, 144, 146, 148,
150, 154, 156, 158, 160, 162, 168, 170, 172, 174, 176, 178, 182
184, 186, 188, 196, 206, 218, 220, 224b, 230

Crysta Rosella Luke– Artist {76}

Crysta is a magnificent young artist in Atlanta, Georgia. Having discovered
her artist's heart, eye, hand, and discipline at a very early age.
She graduated from the Savannah College of Art and
Design with an impressive, and deep body of work.
The mother of two girls, and a business manager,
her vision continues to grow.

Pages: 10, 12, 14, 16t, 22, 24, 26, 28, 30, 32, 34, 36, 38, 40, 42, 44, 46, 50, 52,
54, 56, 58, 60, 62, 64, 66, 70, 72, 74, 76, 78, 82, 84, 86, 90, 92, 94, 96,
98, 100, 104, 106, 110, 112, 114, 116, 118, 120, 122, 130, 134, 138,
140, 142, 144, 148, 150, 152, 154, 156, 160, 162, 166, 168, 170
174, 176, 178, 180, 182, 186, 190, 202, 212t, 216, 230

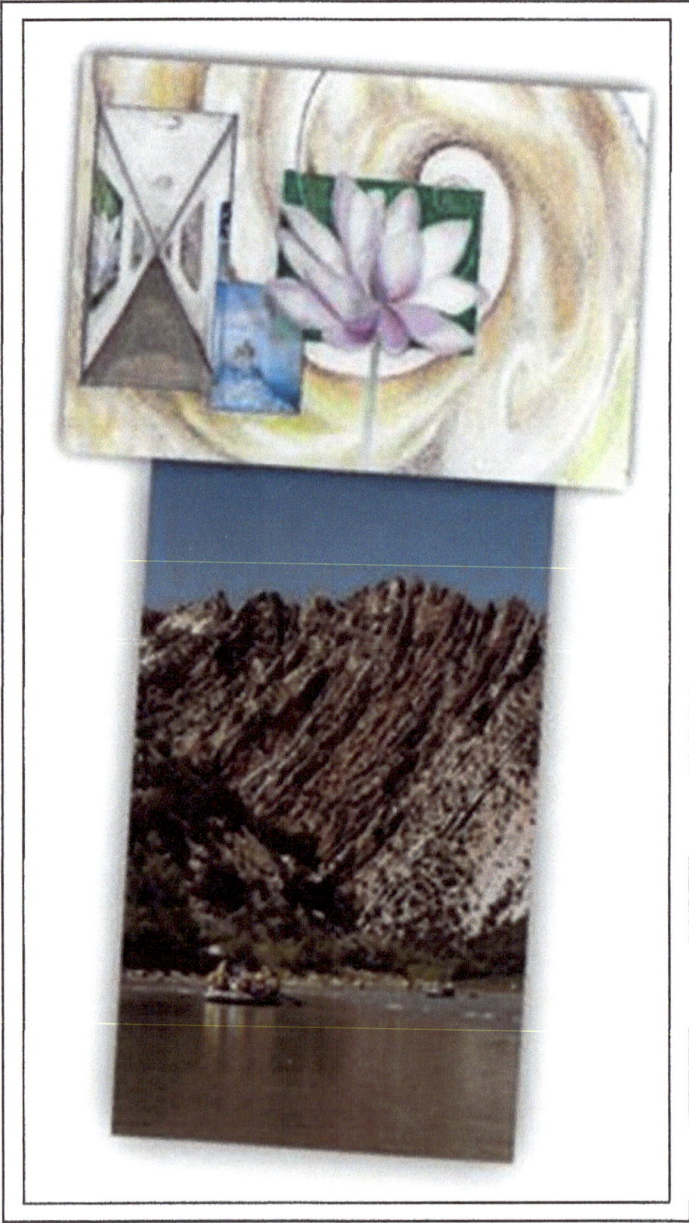

Credits for the Sweet Images (2)

Patricia Ryan Madson – Artist {21}

Patricia is an Emerita of Stanford University where she taught for three decades in the Drama Department. She founded the Stanford Improvisors in 1991, and has spent a happy lifetime leading classes, seminars, and workshops teaching the ease of the creative process, and the magic of improvising.
She currently teaches for
Stanford's Continuing Studies.
IMPROV WISDOM: Don't Prepare, Just Show Up,
was published 2005 by Bell Tower Books, a Random House publication. The book has been published in nine languages, and is available as both audio and e-book. Patricia designs workshops, and keynote presentations for organizations worldwide. Her current passion is 'plein air' watercolor painting.
http://www.improvwisdom.com/Bio.html

Pages: 18, 20, 48t, 80, 88, 108, 124, 128, 132, 164t, 196, , 200t, 204t, 206, 208, 212b, 226, 228, 232t, 234

Sophia Sabsowitz – Artist {16}

Sophia Sabsowitz is an abstract painter living, and working in Atlanta, Georgia. Her paintings capture a psychedelic fusion of colors that take over canvas to create luminous, captivating works reminiscent of ocean waves right before a storm. Recently, her fluid paintings have been exploring the cosmos, and the natural world. Her main materials include glass paints, acrylics, and oil. She uses non-traditional painting techniques including pouring, layering, and hand altering to compose vibrant abstract landscapes. Sophia's color palette draws heavily from her dreams, and emotions.
The Art of Sophia Sabsowitz, Atlanta, GA 2017
https://www.theartofsophiasabsowitz.com/about

Pages: 48b, 102, 126, 136, 146, 158, 164b, 172, 194, 198, 200b, 204b, 210, 214, 222, 232b

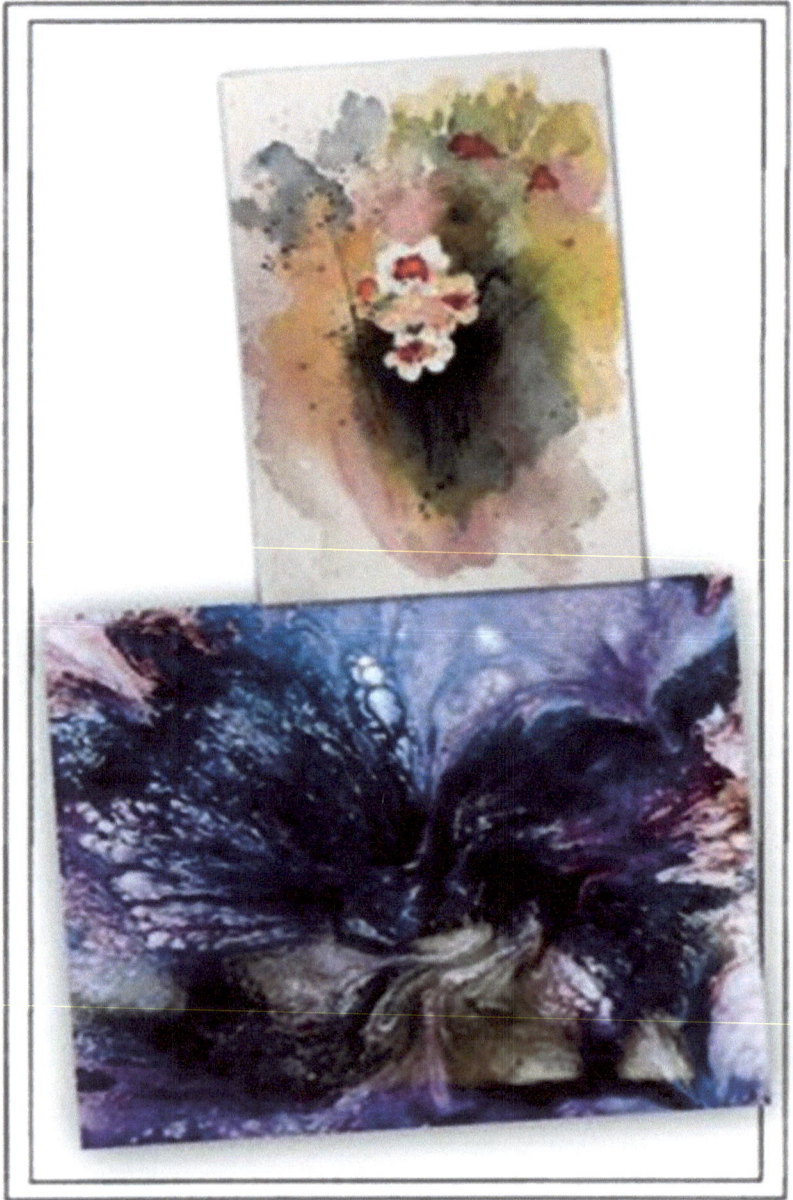

Credits for the Sweet Images (3)

Jonathan Michael Mawle Lowe
Artist, and Photographer

Jonathan's experience includes Yerkes Primate
Center, Emory's Mass Spectrometry Laboratory,
and privately contracted work, with Health Connect South.
A graduate of Aberystwyth University, Wales, Jonathan is a health
Informatics Analyst, Winship Cancer Institute, Emory University, Atlanta, GA

Pages: 184, 188, 218, 236t

Robert Lowe – Photographer {32}

Pages: 3, 18, 20, 30, 32, 80, 92, 102, 114, 120, 124, 132, 136, 152, 166, 180, 190, 192, 194, 198, 202, 208, 210, 214, 216, 220, 222, 224t, 226, 228, 234, 236b,

AnnLisa Sutton – Artist

One of the lovely and talented people from my commune days
detailed in *Happy Vernday Birthcox: Revolution, Evolution, and an
Uncommon Commune – 1970.* Andrea is somewhere in the world.

Page 192

Elizabeth McCormick Bogue – Artist

Elizabeth had 84 years when I met her. I rented a room in her home where
it was revealed that she had been a Red Cross Executive for nearly
40 years, and had turned to watercolor painting in her
elder age. She gave this to me when I last saw her
before she left us in 1996.

Page 16b

Skydive Atlanta - Photograph
http://www.skydiveatlanta.com/

Page 68

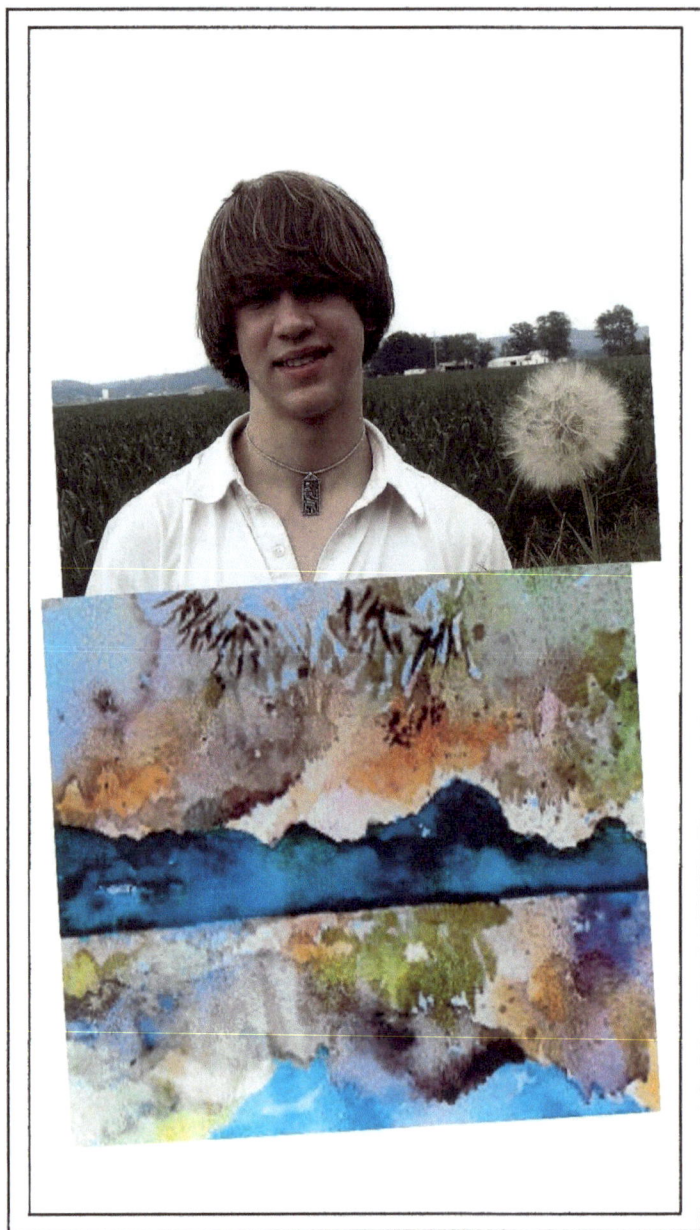

The Author

As a retired Improvisation elder, and lifetime dreamer, my major
professional credential has been as the founder, and chief executive of
Improvisation, Inc., an early educational consulting firm specializing
introducing of the applications of Improvisation, beyond the theater
(philosophy, theory, tools, and techniques) to all areas of human
gathering. In a thirty-eight- year exploration of Improvisation,
It has been a pleasure to have been a dancer, a player, a teacher, a director,
a pioneering Improv Theater founder, Artistic Director, and a mentor.
Work and play in Improvisation is a philosophical basis of my life.
Improvisation, Inc. has been foundational in the development
of the global movement that is exploring, the applications,
pedagogy, professional development, and best
practices of Applied Improvisation,
a young, and rapidly expanding
field of human endeavor.
Lifework has offered many things, from business management,
to teaching at Georgia State University; to having been
a director in a county welfare outpost, a community
organizer, and an Officer in the U.S. Navy.
Ten years were spent in an extraordinary community of communes, social
services, and politics during the time of radical change, between 1970 and 1980.
The full story, is in *Happy Vernday Birthcox: Revolution, Evolution, and an
Uncommon Commune - 1970*, published in 2015. It shares
the extraordinary people and times that opened body,
mind, and spirit to a global perspective, and guided
ultimately to the discovery of Improvisational Dance,
in San Diego, California in 1980, Improvisational Comedy,
and exploration of a life of Applied Improvisation,
and *The Greater Number*.

The Author (2)

My world view has been greatly influenced by the peaceful martial art of Aikido and the rank of *Nidan*, and the status of *Fuku Shidoin* (teacher). Twenty-two years on the mat, seven years specializing in teaching children, has grounded my universal viewpoint in a both a physical, and a deeply spiritual world. My articles have been published in "The Journal of Asian Martial Arts", and "Aikido Today Magazine". An influence on my world that has driven the journey to *The Greater Number* is having grown up in a ghettoized neighborhood which had one of the highest juvenile crime rates in America between, 1950 and 1970. There were youth gangs before they became fashionable, with an infamous motorcycle gang headquarters down the block. There I learned to walk in a very centered awareness, and a deep need to always be on search for grander horizons. While in college I worked in poverty communities in South Central Los. Through years of disruption, massive change, revolution, and evolution, we have come to the time of learning ourselves; seeking to find real, personal, internal, and creative human engagement that can lead both to freedom, and to full expression of the individual, and fully engaged collaboration among us all. In retirement, much time is spent in contemplation and meditation, some time spent each day playing a musical instrument, much writing, reading, delighting in the beauty and abundance of this life, and in grateful thanks to God for all that is, including the most profound influence, my fine young son, who now has 30 years, and is the delight of my life.

www.ingramcontent.com/pod-product-compliance
Lightning Source LLC
Chambersburg PA
CBHW042000090426
42811CB00031B/1968/J